Unrested Peace

Jason Stanton

Published by
French Point Publishing
Webb City, MO 64870
www.frenchpointpublishing.wordpress.com

Front cover: Courtesy of the author.
Back cover: Jason Stanton

All images are by the author unless otherwise noted

First published 2014
Manufactured in the United States

ISBN: 978-0615989167

Library of Congress Cataloging-in-Publication Data
Stanton, Jason
Unrested Peace / Jason Stanton
p. cm.

ISBN: 978-0615989167
1.   Paranormal-Ghosts-Haunting-Biography

Note: The information in this book is true and complete to the best of our knowledge. It is offered without guidance on the part of the author or French Point Publishing. The author and French Point Publishing disclaim all liability in connection with the use of this book.

Introduction:

Growing up with one brother and three sisters was rough. I'm sure that our parents had their hands full and were not financially stable. I do believe that some of the pain I endured was a symptom of the stress that must have been on their minds. My education was lacking and my self-esteem was not the best; but learning coping skills to achieve my goals and dreams was a task that although hard to do, became easy to follow.

I didn't have the fancy clothes or the best supplies unlike most kids around me. Most of my possessions were second- hand or passed down from other relatives. Going to school, I knew that I wasn't wealthy and didn't fit into the million-dollar lifestyle that inhabited most of society that called Goshen, New York home. Other hobbies such as playing my guitar, writing lyrics, hanging out in cemeteries, and even smoking marihuana filled my lonely days to avoid the pain and torment that my peers put me through regularly.

Feeling alone and isolated, I felt that I would do anything I could, even breaking the law would help put a smile on my face. When I moved into the house out on Quarry Road about five miles from town I was disappointed and angry; leaving behind the many things that I had access to on a daily basis, such as the library. Not expecting that the events to come, and emotions, including love, worry, heartbreak, and knowledge of the physical and paranormal world would flip my life upside-down; helping me learn that there are more important things about which to worry. I knew that people can be cruel and hurtful, and it doesn't matter. The only thing that mattered was how I viewed myself and what I wanted to achieve. That is a lesson that is rough to learn but no one can ever take away. That lesson is what will drive you to be successful in every dream.

I don't look back with regret or hate nor will I ever do so. I've learned to let go and move forward with what I have, and do what I can. I gain knowledge on paranormal phenomena as well as a peaceful lifestyle. If anything is taken from my story I can only hope that it is these words.

Most of my childhood was spent alone and at times was like living in a world isolated by iron bars that would be found in some prison such as Alcatraz:

The summer of 1991: I am 14; a sophomore in high school and nowhere near being one of the popular kids. To be honest I get picked on a lot. Maybe because I am overweight or I have long blond hair and blue eyes and listen to heavy metal music; or maybe it's the ripped jeans, but I think it is more because I choose not follow what everyone expects of me. I assume that I will be voted the most likely to not succeed by all my classmates.

I am a curious kid and spend a lot of time at the library reading books by Stephen King, and anything on human development. I am more than curious about the subject. To sit and think of how electrons pulsate through our nervous system controlling everything from body movement to thought is fascinating.

It's summer and school is out. The days are hot, reaching temperatures of 101, and the sun shows no mercy as the days go along. My parents work long days and I hardly ever seen them so I always find creative ways to keep my mind occupied like reading or building a club house. I love playing football and playing guitar as well as smoking pot. I have a crush on a girl in school named Jill Renzo. She has long black hair, smooth flawless skin, small waist, probably about a C cup and stands about 5'5. Boy is she gorgeous. I don't think she knows that I exist, but I can tell that we would get along just fine. She wears those cute ripped jeans, and denim skirts, and t-shirts that force me to use my imagination on how perky her cute nipples must be. I've had many fantasies with her, whether on top or from behind; either way they always ended well.

I have one brother named Will and 3 sisters' Karen, Lyn, and Jean. Jean is the only one that's younger than me, by 5 years. The others are older and don't like me too much, always joining the festivities with everyone else while shouting out names at me that would make the average person tear up. It bothers me and makes me feel as though I am beneath them, but it also makes me want to strive harder to be more self-sufficient, as they spend their days hanging out with their friends and picking on me.

Even though I am always told I will never succeed and am called names such as fat ass, lazy prick, dumb shit, and other obscure adjectives, I keep my head high. I know that one day I will be something special. I keep up researching human development and behavior patterns learning things such as that beta-waves range between 13-40 HZ. The beta state is associated with peak concentration, heightened alertness and visual acuity, alpha-waves range between 7-12 HZ. This is a place of deep relaxation, but not quite a meditative state. Theta-waves range between 4-7 HZ. The theta state is one of the more elusive and-extraordinary realms to explore. It is also known as the twilight state, which we normally only experience fleetingly as we rise up out of the depths of delta state upon waking. It always makes me curious wondering if only we could control these waves at will what would happen and how would it affect our actions, and whether or not we could transmit those waves outside our body.

I also spend a lot of time in cemeteries reviewing my own outlook on life. It is really soothing and peaceful; a moment of self-indulged hypnosis. I just like staring at the headstones reading about the beings that once walked this planet, and imagining what kind of person they each were in life. I wonder what happens to their spirit. Is there a heaven or a hell and is it as described by many theological scholars? At night I love looking up at the sky hoping that I will catch sight of a meteor shower or some kind of star that I've never seen before and I get lost in my thoughts wondering about different universes and dimensions. What would it be like to travel through space and move at the speed of light? What questions could be answered just by spending a day up there and looking through a solar system that hasn't been explored?

My hometown of Goshen, New York is a small town. Most of the buildings were built in the mid-1800s, with some dating to the 1700s. Very little renovation has been done so it still looks as it would have 150 years ago, with the exception of the paved roads. Population hovers around 15,000 or so. The cemetery I go to a lot, called Slate Hill Cemetery, (why they chose that name I never knew because Slate Hill is about 25 miles away), is outside of town, on a little back road behind the horse track. It isn't a very big place, just a few hundred grave stones, some dating back to the 1760s, which I think is pretty cool. The cemetery sits on a small hill which, from a distance, looks like a grassy knoll that you've only read about in a fantasy novel written for a teenage girl audience. I spend a lot of afternoons here just talking to myself and smoking an occasional joint until well past sundown. I know I am not supposed to be here this late, but I really don't care. I find this place peaceful and relaxing, which helps me be more centered in a safe environment.

I've never really believed in ghosts or spirits, nor am I really religious. I've never thought that religion made any sense, and I have too many unanswered questions about it to be a believer. I cannot understand following a faith based on a book written by man. How can one say that it is the word of God? Or explain how different priests and ministers will tell you what the words mean? Other the ten commandants the writings are obscure, and in my eyes, mean only what the person interpreting them believes. The idea of ghosts also leaves me questioning, and although I have no knowledge that they do exist, I can't say that they don't exist either. I often wonder whether or not they exist, but feel that science would have answered this question by now if there was proof of their existence.

Sometimes I stop at a church on my way home and light one candle, saying a little prayer to those who have passed from this land. Why I do this? I never know, it just feels like a good thing to do out of respect. This Catholic Church is a more modern one built from standard bricks that would have been commonly found in the 60s or 70s. It also serves as a pre-school and holds other classes for young minds who want to become closer to the Heavenly Father.

I'm not always the best kid and I have gotten into my share of trouble; typical teenage things like stealing from stores, loitering, as well as trespassing. I have never been violent and hardly ever raise my voice to anyone. I don't think it is necessary. I just move on and avoid the confrontation.

This summer my mom signed me up for Boy Scouts, for what reason I have no idea. It just doesn't seem to fit my personality at all, but I thought why not give it a shot. We have to meet on Tuesday nights down at the V.F.W. I was very uncomfortable at my first meeting; everyone was dressed wearing those stupid plain green and brown clothes looking like we all just escaped from jail. My troop leader is an older fellow, probably in his mid-50s, grey hair, slightly taller than me, very stern with a bad attitude which I don't like at all. I've never gotten along with authority figures. I become rebellious toward them, but for some reason this time I played along.

I learned the Scout slogan or code, whatever the fuck they want to call it. It doesn't matter to me at all right now. We regularly take hiking trips to different parts of the state where we learn how to use different knot-tying techniques, use of a compass, dowsing rods to find water, how to kill our own food if necessary, and building shelters, which I have to say, is pretty cool. Sure, I don't fit in with the others at all being an outcast....

Chapter 1:

The House

It's August: I just got word from my parents that we have to move and I am worried. I have become accustomed to this small town and enjoy being able to go to the library and the cemetery. I have made a home out of those places, and what if we left town altogether and I never have the opportunity to see Jill again or tell her what I think?

The idea of moving has definitely left me worried about many things. I am not ready to give up this town that I am now proud to call home.

I'm spending more time than usual in the cemetery and staring at the stars wondering if I will have to change my life again, to fit a new environment. I often stare at the compass my parents bought me for boy scouts hoping that it would point me in the right direction (a quirky thought considering it will always point due north because of the magnetic pull of the earth).

We are moving out into the farm region of Goshen. It is awesome to know that I am still going to be in the same school district, so seeing Jill again won't be a problem, but 10 miles away from the cemetery and the library...?

The school year is approaching fast and I am eager and a bit exited to see this new place. Being in the farm land area, I imagine a lot of black dirt and corn fields as well as old farm houses standing one or two stories high. I didn't sleep well at all the last few days in our small apartment, wondering what exactly I am going to do out there to keep my mind at ease.

It's the last week of August and we have started to move. The day is the hottest of the whole summer, I think, reaching a temperature of 108. The sweat is beading and running down my forehead and chunky stomach. I watch as my home town becomes smaller and further away from my sight as we drive away. I quietly say goodbye to the town I grew fond of, even though I'm only moving ten miles away. I feel so far away from home. I try to think of this as a new chapter in my life. I am just not sure how or where to start this next journey, in what I imagine to be, a new desolate area.

I watch civilization pass behind the car, as we head farther into the woods. I think to myself where is all the farm land that I heard about; the corn, carrots, and cows? I don't see any of that at all. We drive down a road where I see one farm, with an old, typical 1880s farm house, and with one good sized cornfield that has been well taken care of; the ears at least a foot long, the stalks well over six feet tall. We now turn off that road, and pull into the very first driveway on the left. I have an idea of where I am at, but I have never explored this part of town.

The driveway leads to a two-story, stone building that appears as though it hasn't been lived in for many years. My parents tell me that it needs some serious cleaning and work done. My first thought is that an atomic bomb couldn't fix this house. There is moss growing up the side of the building, and the roof above the garage doesn't look as though it will last another year. Some of the windows are broken, and the front porch where a tall pine tree stands has paint that is chipping, the screens are ripped, and the floor boards are busted; exposing some of the rotted rafters underneath. Woods surround the house and most spots are pretty thick though I can see another farm down the road. The grass in the yard is about five-foot high and thick as the Amazon jungle. There is an old shed on the right side of the backyard, made of ply-wood and two-by-fours that is partially collapsed. The driveway is cracked and in need of some serious patch work.

I walk inside hoping that it looks better than the outside, but it doesn't change my first impression. The walls are faded and worn and the floorboards are loose and coming up, although holding a shiny finish. There are bags of clothes and garbage all over the place.

I ask my dad, "How on earth we are going to make this livable by the end of the weekend?"

To myself I think *'Sure I am a bit handy, but there's no way we can do this.'*

Dad smiles, "No worries, we will do one thing at a time."

Dad backs his truck up to the door and we begin hauling out bags of trash and debris. *My God, there better be something in this area that will make the stay worth it.*

As the day goes on we take six truckloads of junk to the dump and the first floor is starting to look like something livable. The kitchen is of good size and easily accommodates our twelve-foot table, with plenty of room to walk around. The windows are tall, and I decide I can easily fit my fat butt through without many issues. The door to the basement is in the kitchen as well. I haven't explored the basement yet. The other side of the kitchen is open, leading to the dining room on one side, and the living room on the other side.

The living room has some brown shag and frayed carpeting with six windows, which are just as big as in the kitchen. There is a stone fireplace, built caddy-cornered up against the wall that separates the living room from the dining room. The rest of that wall is 12 inch by 12 inch mirrors and the center mirror has a picture of a lion on it with brilliant blue and purple. It sure is beautiful, but I wonder why anyone would do that in a living room. The dining room is all oak; stained beautifully with ornate engravings and built-in shelves. The craftsman who did the work must have of been proud of his accomplishment. There is only one door which leads to the broken porch. The staircase to second floor is also in the dining room. The banister is also well-crafted, ornate stained wood with spindles that were precisely carved in some kind of art deco design. *This place could really be something that I love.*

I start walking up the stairs to the second floor, one step at a time, admiring the wood work. Half way up there is a two-foot octagon stained glass window. It has a design that I can't quite place, but looks like it belongs in a historical church that I once saw exploring in town. I reach the top of the stairs which open onto a long hallway, lined with doors on each side, four on the right and three on the left. The paint on the walls is cracked and I wonder whether it is lead-based. The floor feels stable and does not seem to bend under my slow steps, although I hear the boards creak. I open each door slowly, not knowing what I will find behind them, but half expecting an animal to jump out at any moment.

The bedrooms are fairly clean, so I spend most of my time scraping down the walls getting rid of the old paint. The rooms are large, so I'm pretty sure there will not be any fighting over who gets what room. I've worked on the upstairs cleaning and chipping for hours now, and am getting excited to start getting my stuff moved up here. I choose the first room on the left as my bedroom, which overlooks the huge pine tree in the front yard. I decide to paint my room a dark blue because I like the contrast in color to the sun shining in. I have to two windows in my room, original to when the house was built.

I spend the next three hours cleaning the dust and dirt from my windows and floor. I set my bed up facing the wall that has the staircase on the other side and my dresser is against that wall with my stereo sitting on top. I spend the next couple days sitting in my room playing my guitar, taking in the atmosphere of the new house.

My mind wanders to ponder that the end of the summer is approaching quickly and school will be starting in another week. Thankfully, I am still in the same school and I am eagerly waiting to see Jill's beautiful smile again. I haven't been outside much to explore what could be around the house. I have been mostly cleaning up and helping to fix what was needed to be repaired. It has been a long day and I know that I need some sun and exercise. I walk outside staring at the tall grass in the yard. *There is no way an average lawn mower is going to cut all this down to a more respectable height.*

I walk into the woods a few hundred yards and discover what appears to be a scrap metal graveyard. As I look around, my eyes settle on the king of this graveyard: an old GM car that is still in fairly good shape. *The motor has to be seized up being on the front line of what Mother Nature has been throwing this way.*

Even so, I still find a little enjoyment out of hopping in the car and pretending that I am a race car driver. Losing interest, I explore further. On the far side of the mounds of scrap metal is an old, dilapidated, concrete foundation, but to what? The concrete blocks stand ten feet high at one end and narrow in height as the slope of the ground rises higher until it is flush with the blocks. It doesn't look like the foundation to a house. *Why on earth is this here and what was the purpose?* There is not any other evidence, just some fallen trees.

Chapter 2:

The Cemetery

I walk back to the house accompanied by the sound of my stomach growling. I feel like I haven't eaten anything in a week. I'm not sure if Mom has gone food shopping, but I need to find something to put in my belly.

I walk through my front door and begin searching the cabinets, and pour a big bowl of cereal. I sit in the living room and pop Fantasia from Walt Disney into the VCR. The first piece of music is beginning when I get an urge to smoke a fat joint. I go outside and feel the cool air blowing in from the east. *The seasons are starting to change.* I always love autumn. I walk back inside and lie down on the couch with my eyes glued to the TV. There is something about classical music that I love. It is very soothing.

As evening sets in, the air is feeling cold; but I am not sure why or how. The temperature outside is in the 60s, but in the house it feels as though it is in the 30s. *Old building, drafty or whatever.*

The mirror -covered wall starts to look odd, twisting pale shades of gray with a yellow tint, where silver had been earlier. The lion that previously filled the center mirror with vibrant blue and purple now looks pale, and appears to be staring at me. I speak to it a few times in laughter, making a silly face. *Stop looking at me.*

Shortly before the end of the movie, I hear a thump from the dining room that has now been turned into a game room. My parents put a pool table in the center of the room; a couple of dart boards on the wall, and beer lights that hung from the center of the ceiling. I walk into the game room and notice that a book has fallen off of a shelf. *It's just an old house and the shelves aren't level.* Regardless, enough is enough for tonight and I walk upstairs to bed.

*****

I wake up late, close to noon. I go downstairs to get a cup of coffee. The incident from last night is still racing through my head. I go back upstairs with my coffee and pop a Metallica cassette into the stereo. I am not sure what happened, but.... *It must have been the pot I smoked. Maybe I should call my dealer and ask what exactly it was that he sold me.*

I assure myself that between a long day of moving and the pot, that my mind is playing tricks on me. *I need some more fresh air.*

I go outside and decide to explore again. I head in the opposite direction from where I went yesterday. Through the woods, I come across a path about eight feet wide. I turn up it, admiring all the colors that are filling the trees, from bright yellows, reds to some with a sun burst effect. I notice a clearing up ahead, and curiosity fills my mind. *Where does this wide path lead?* I have a form of excitement that is rushing through me like nothing I have ever felt before. As I get closer, I notice tall mounds of stones and conveyer belts, among the trees. This seems a bit odd to be in the middle of the woods. I start running faster toward it.

When I reach the mounds of stones and equipment, I realize that I am no longer in the middle of the woods, but instead I am next to main the road, at least a mile away from my house. I am smack dead in the middle of the rock quarry that is on that road. I start to walk around the quarry and it looks as though these conveyer belts and trucks have not operated in a long time. The quarry is deserted, equipment dusty with stone fragments still on the conveyors, as if the workers walked away without notice. The belts have so many splices I would be shocked if they could carry any rocks. The paint on the machines is faded and cracked and in need of serious maintenance. *They must have closed for the summer?* I climb up on one of the belts and hang my feet over the side as I sit down. I watch as wild animals come through the woods to the center of the quarry. I scan the scene while up there. There are trucks parked to the back side next to a small shack.

On the east side of the quarry is a flat surface with a big rock face probably about a hundred foot tall. It looks like that is where they were blasting to get stone. I get off the belt and start walking, continuing along the path. I admire the bright colors of the maple, oak and spruce trees that once were green. The woods look peaceful and I feel as if nothing else matters as I continue my journey. I notice a stream on the right side of me. The sound of the water trickling down the rocks sounds is so soothing. On the other side of the stream stands a deer. His fur has begun to darken with the approaching winter. He stares at me for what seems an hour, but which I am sure was only a few moments. His tail is hidden between his hind legs as he glares at me, with a look of concern and fear. He lowers his head to take another bite of the grass that he has been grazing on when I take a step and break a twig on the ground. He is startled and runs. From this distance I hear a couple more animals scurry in the underbrush, perhaps watching as the deer took the risk of becoming visible to human sight.

I continue down the path a few hundred yards and notice a small building with red shingles in the distance. I walk faster, wondering why this building is in the middle of the woods. I approach the building from the back. It cannot be bigger than a single ten by ten room. It is a stone structure, much like my house, and has moss on the north side. It has no windows and my curiosity to find out what it is, intensifies with each step. I walk to the front of the building where I see a steel door, reinforced with quarter-inch steel plate. The door is chained shut with a big padlock, as well as a dead bolt. *This is pretty odd, what the hell is something like this doing in the middle of the woods.*

I take a step back and scan the front of the building from top to bottom. There are words engraved in the top plate of steel: "KEEP OUT DANGER HIGH EXPLOSIVES". *I really want in! This must be where the quarry keeps its T.N.T.*

I try the doors but they don't budge. After my brief tug of war, I give up and continue my walk up to the rock face. I arrive at the top of the hill about fifteen minutes later and pierce the thick of the woods, stepping onto the flat clearing on top of the cliff face. I know I have to be careful.

One false move will cause a rock slide. *I don't want to get hurt.*

I slowly make my way out to the edge trying to feel every vibration through my feet. I look down and it seems a lot farther of a drop then I thought when seen from below. I feel as though I am king of the world. The cool fall air is grazing the back of my neck, the sun is sinking low to the west and the sky is filled with brilliant colors from orange, red, purple, blue. I have never felt so tranquil in my life.

I sit down on the edge. Without consciously realizing, I begin reviewing my life and the direction it is headed. School is starting in just days and I can make a fresh start with a positive impact. I am tired of being picked on and treated like shit as though I am worthless. *How will I approach Jill and tell her she is beautiful and smart, and that I adore her. Why am I treated like crap. I've even lied for people so they would not get into trouble. Why is the world being so cruel at times?*

I pull my compass out of my pocket, hoping it will point in the direction that I should go, but of course north is where it points me.

It is getting late and the sun is almost below the horizon. At the same time, the moon is already high, beautiful and glowing pure white. I awaken from my trance on top of that wall and head for home with a joint in my hand. My pot supply is getting low and I need to make a phone call to get more. The trail is getting real dark and a bit eerie. My mind is racing, and I begin thinking that something is behind me but I can see nothing but the dark trees. I pick up my pace hoping that I will not trip over underbrush, now invisible in the growing darkness. I can almost hear footsteps following me. I hear branches breaking and what sounds like heavy breathing gaining ground on me. It sounds close and I have begun to run, when I hear my mom yelling in the distance.

I show up at my doorstep at about 10 p.m. unharmed and safe. I have no idea what was following me, and I do not really want to find out. *It was probably some kind of animal that could have of eaten me for dinner.* I am suddenly exhausted, every last bit of energy drained from me, barely able to stand. I pass on food and just head to bed.

It is a strange dream, and is about my old house.

It was dark and I was out in the woods behind the house getting warm from the cold winter around a campfire. I don't know why I was in the woods. I have only hung out there few times because it is short cut to my school. I sit with my hands held over the flames and watch them flicker and dance into my palms.

The night was cold and the stars were bright. The moon was full, red as the blood that flowed in my veins. There was movement all around me, but for some reason I paid no attention to it. I could feel the vibration through my toes as the ground around me was vibrating with fury. Several shadows danced at the tree line, moving from tree to tree as if they were trying to hide. I could hear laughter and crying all at once. Pure chaos. There was a strange mist that glowed close to the ground, which was matted of leaves. I saw a dead animal in the distance but could not determine what kind of creature. It was covered in flies, and I could sense the sadness that it must have of felt before it had reached that last breath. The dancing shadows were getting closer and I could almost make out their features. They were nothing that I had ever seen. They did not have a defined shape, but rather changed over and over, from one life form to another and another....

"Jason!" My mom is yelling at me.

"What"

"Its 2 p.m."

"Ok." I cannot believe I slept that long, nearly fourteen hours.

I go down stairs to get my coffee and use the bathroom. I look outside. The wind has done some damage to the leaves as they are falling from the trees more rapidly than expected. I am not prepared for the winter, and even less so for school, which was starts in a couple days. I feel nervous.

I go back up to my room and stare out the window for a bit. The needles on the spruce tree are even falling off, and I can see what is across the street much clearer. I haven't gone off in those woods yet or even thought about going. Through the trees I notice something a bit odd. There are stones that sit a few inches off the ground in perfect rows and columns.

I get dressed and go out to have a closer look. I trample through the 'pricker' bushes and black cap bushes, till I get to the spot where the stones sit. I am in an area where the trees are spaced further apart. There are broken limbs and tree trunks lying on the ground. The ground is matted heavily with tree needles, and the sun can barely pierce the top of the trees. I can smell the odor of decaying limbs and wet leaves. I walk slowly.

"Oh fuck!" I just tripped over something. I look back and notice a stone sticking out of the ground. I get up closer to inspect it, only a few inches tall, it has a small arch on top and is outlined in what looks like marble or soapstone. *What the fuck is this...?*

Now it hits me. "It's a fucking headstone. Oh my god," I whisper for no one to hear.

I start to dig around the stone so I can read the inscription. I dig down about a foot and can see what at one time were words, but the weather and time have eroded them to the point of obscurity, just as the stone itself had been swallowed by the ground as it slowly sank from view. *Are there more headstones?* I search the ground, looking past the fallen needles. Again I feel exited over this new territory. I can't believe that I have stumbled across a cemetery in the middle of nowhere. I wonder why this spot for a cemetery, and who is buried here. I count altogether seventy headstones, and I am sure that more may be completely buried. I have found a new place to hang out, besides the rock wall. I am excited that this is only a few hundred feet from my doorstep.

Chapter 3:

My Crazy Sister

It is the day before my first day of school and I feel extremely on edge. I am worried about all the typical bullshit that comes with dealing with my peers. I know that I am going to be called names and pushed around, as always. I promise myself that I will not let them bother me. I know that I am better than what I am given credit for, and I am destined to do great things. I just am not sure what those great things will be.

I sit in my room today. The weather is unseasonably cold for this time of the year. Winter is blowing down our back quickly and relentlessly. I have been thinking about the odd things that I have been feeling over the course of the past couple weeks; from feeling like the mirror was staring at me, to being followed in the woods coming home, and that weird dream that I had about the dancing shadows at our old house. I do not know why all these things are happening, and I know it is not normal. I try to convince myself that it is the added stress of starting a new school year, or maybe it is from the pot I have been smoking. Maybe it is stress from my parents, who are being their typical, demanding selves, as usual. They want me to weed whack the half acre of grass that is over grown in the yard, before snow starts to fall. They also want me to help cut firewood, and stack it on the porch which looks as though it will not hold a small dog, much less a couple ricks of wood. We have not even cleaned that porch yet, with discarded things scattered over it.

I need more coffee before I start in on that list of chores. I don't have much time to finish, and I know that it will take more than a day to finish the list. I fill the weed whacker with mixed fuel (one part 2 cycle oil to a gallon of gas) and start on the far end of the yard. It becomes obvious that this is not a one day job as I thrust the machine side to side cutting down the tall grass to about ankle level. Even after I'm done, I decide that it will still need to be mowed, and will then take a few weeks before it will look good.

I continue cutting grass, getting lost in my thoughts with a pair of headphones on wired to my Walkman. I swipe at the grass, imagining that I am god taking revenge on a small village. It keeps my mind occupied enough to make the day to go by quickly. As I approach the halfway point I get sprayed with blood. Spots cover my face and more across my pants. *What was that!* I kneel down to find out what I hit and notice blades of grass shaking about a foot ahead of me. I push the grass away from side to side curious as to what crossed my path. As I do so, within inches of my hand I see a long dark brown tail, quivering in the grass. I grab and slowly pull it toward me. Inch by inch, it gets closer and more recognizable.

"Holy fuck! A copperhead! *Highly poisonous.*

I don't like the idea of killing animals. I've always thought that every living creature deserved to live with pride; to be honest humans should be considered more of a bad species than this snake that was just trying to survive. I come along and destroy it.

I pick a spot on the far end of the yard to bury the creature. I dig a hole about two feet down, place it inside and cover it up. I make a little cross out of sticks to mark the grave. I say a little prayer because it feels like the right thing to do.

I give up weed whacking for the evening. Half of the yard is done and I decide that I will finish it the following weekend. I start to clean out the porch on the front of the house getting it ready for the firewood. The outside porch door is wedged shut; pushing and pulling on it does nothing.

I cut a hole in the screen on the side of the porch and climb through the opening. I will have to fix the hole later but for now I hope to see why the door wasn't opening. I look around and do not see anything obstructing the door. I grab a hold of the handle and pull it toward me and open the door with ease. *What the fuck is going on here.* I pause for a few minutes even more confused than before.

I start throwing things into the back of my dad's old beat up pickup truck. Most of it is old sporting equipment like fishing poles, hiking gear etc. I know that the owners live in the city and my parents are renting the house. The owners lived here when they were kids and were obviously outdoor adventurers. I can probably use some of this stuff. I love hiking, camping and fishing. All in all I threw it in the truck.

As I get closer to the back wall, I uncover a stack of boxes. I open them up and shuffle through the hundreds of books that fill them. I look at titles from some of the best authors of the 70s and 80s. I pick out some of the better horror and suspense novels and place them aside in a separate stack. The back side of the porch has another full size door that was covered from view from inside the porch just hours before. I wonder where this door leads. I slowly open the door to see a total black space. Now I am extremely curious to find out where this leads. I cannot see anything. Feeling along the wall for a light switch, I come up empty.

I go back into the main house to get a flashlight out of the junk drawer in the kitchen and put some batteries in it. Now I rush back to the door.

I slowly open it and turn on the flashlight, I feel like a kid at Christmas wondering what present I just found. I shine the light across the dark space, and it reflects off of what appears to be car parts or bike parts. It appears to be an oversized closet that is about twelve feet deep and about five feet wide. There is a light in the center with a pull chord dangling from the fixture. I climb over the crap and scrape my shin on what I think is a motor. I feel a little bit of blood run down my leg.

I make my way to the string and pull. The light does not come on. I decide to finish cleaning the main porch, thinking that I will get a new bulb after I get back from the dump. I hop in the truck with my dad and we set off to unload the truck. It is around 4:30 p.m.

It turned out to be a long trip to the dump. My dad kept lecturing me and belittling me about what I choose to do in my free time. I kept asking what difference does it makes, I'm not hurting anyone or anything. I love hanging out in cemeteries, reading, and nature walks. He does not like the idea of me sticking up for myself. My dad is strict and wants me to spend my free time working. *So he doesn't have to.* I don't mind helping out and doing things around the house but I don't think that I should have to dedicate every free moment to being treated like a servant. I get a little loud with him, and he smacks me alongside my face. I shrug it off knowing it isn't the first and won't be the last time I get hit. Now my face is starting to bruise slightly. *This is a great way to go to school on the first day. He is a total fucking dickhead.*

We get back home about 6:00 p.m. I eagerly get a light bulb to put in the fixture in that closet. I am eager to get a good look at all the contents.

I stumble back over the parts and screw in the new bulb. When I pull the string, light brightens the closet. I notice that shelves surround the edges of the closet, and on top is everything from old candles, books, and old tools. On the back wall of the closet hangs a crucifix. I haven't seen anything religious with the possible exception of the stained glass window in the middle of the stairs. I go through everything in the closet, and stack the trash out on the porch, ready to go to the dump the following weekend.

My mom made grilled cheese sandwiches and tomato soup for dinner tonight. I know it is a bit of a "cheesy" type of dinner but I still love the hell out of a good grilled cheese sandwich.

I sit in the living room next to my oldest sister, Karen. She is your typical blond, not too bright, and easy to mess with her head. Her eyes are pinned to the TV as if the host of whatever talk show she was watching was going to reach through the screen and kiss her.

I pick up the phone and yell at her. "Karen, Karen!"

"What Jay?"

"You have a phone call."

She picks up the phone with excitement speaking loudly in the receiver "Hello, Hello." I start to laugh knowing that the phone never rang and all she got was a dial tone. She chuckled at that too knowing that I had just pulled a prank and said "Jay that's messed up".

A few moments go by when she looks at me and says "Come here a minute, I want to talk to you about something."

I hesitate, not knowing what she has up her sleeve because of the phone prank I just played on her, but I get up and walk closer to the couch that she is sitting on.

Sensing no retaliation, I sit next to her only a few inches away. She leans over and speaks in a soft, concerned voice which is odd for her. She is twenty-years old and has a son of her own.

She quietly asks me, "Have you noticed anything odd that has been happening?"

"Like what?"

Karen starts telling me a story that had happened the night before when she was sitting at the kitchen table having a snack. "It was still pretty early in the morning, around 4am. The room got cold rather quickly and the air felt as though a thick fog had moved in but there was no fog."

She pauses before continuing, "I heard rustling in the game room and it sounded like a few people were having a conversation. I couldn't make out the words but definitely sounded human. I was sitting in the chair and an electric charge ran up my spine. I could hardly breathe and felt paralyzed in the chair."

Karen is serious, and I don't take this as a joke. She even looks a bit scared as she retells what happened. "Then I noticed in the distance of the living room something was moving past the windows, blocking the moonlight from entering. And I got scared. Then also from the living room there were footsteps coming closer to me." My sister is now looking around us as if to see if anyone was suddenly here.

She leans even closer. "I yelled for whatever it was to go away, but it didn't. It moved faster. As it got closer I saw the silhouette of a man with grizzly beard and an overcoat. He looked about as tall as you. It kept coming but by the time it reached the kitchen it had just disappeared. Jay, there is something in this house that we should be afraid of."

I resist my first instinct to say where on earth did you get your weed, because I want a hit. Instead, I share the few strange things I have noticed, including the strange changes with the mirror wall, feeling I was being followed outside, and the odd dream that I had, also last night. I also show her the crucifix in the closet that hangs as if it has a purpose there.

"Makes you wonder if there is a connection between the crucifix and the stuff going on. I kinda think it is just the pot I've been smoking lately. But with that happening to you, I will be more than happy to pay attention more to what is going on around me." I hope I'm assuring her.

She shakes her head, "You're crazy to wanna find out more about these strange things. I will have no part of it."

I understand how she feels, but I have never been a guy to leave my mind wondering about unanswered questions. I always want to test things to see what can happen.

Chapter 4:

Next Witness

Today is the first day of school. I woke feeling unmotivated. I know what I am in for, and am not looking forward to it. I'm making wagers with myself of when 'fat ass', 'dirtbag' or another name is going to be shouted at me. Homeroom, lunch? Still I have to go through it.

I am excited about seeing Jill and getting to the library. I have a lot of things on my mind about ghosts and spirits I want to look up and read. I already spent part of the early morning reading the bible, hoping to find some kind of answer.

It is the human spirit that gives us a consciousness, sense of self, and other remarkable, though limited, "God-like" qualities. The human spirit includes our intellect, emotions, fears, passions, and creativity. It is this spirit that provides us the unique ability to comprehend and understand (Job 32:8, 18). I took those words in as I read them over and over. For something that is said to be against searching for spirits, it did have something to say about their existence. I continued to read more, wondering what more could be in there that would help me understand. I want to learn more about this. The bible mentions heaven, and a hell as place where our souls would suffer for our sins, but what about the middle place, what about Purgatory? What is Purgatory?

After spending the last hour searching for this answer I learned that this teaching is based on the belief that the souls of the dead, who died repentant, but with some punishment remaining for their sins, must be purified through suffering before going to heaven and meeting God. Purgatory is believed to be the temporary state or location, after death, where a person's purification from the guilt and stain of sin occurs. Maybe this is the basis for what is going on here? I'm not sure, but I am determined to find out. This wasn't much to go by, mostly faith and an idea. I am not religious, nor do I want to pretend to be, but it is the only clue that I have right now.

It is starting to get late this morning and I have to venture off to the bottom of the road to catch the bus. I hesitantly close the book and place it on the shelf. I want so bad to bring it with me to school so I can try to and find out more, but I know the other kids would tear me apart if they found out that I had a bible in my bag.

I made it to the bus stop about five minutes before the bus arrived and used that time to smoke a joint and a cigarette. I have no idea what other kids were going to be on this bus, being my first time riding it.

The bus came to a slow halt just a few feet from me. I took a deep breath and did what I could to erase all the bad images and thoughts that raced through my imagination about how this day was going to turn out. I have on my jean jacket, a Suicidal Tendencies t-shirt and my normal ripped jeans, at the knees, as if my parents never bought me school clothes. I just like them because it gave me a little bit more room in the legs. I walk up the steps to the bus and scan the different groups that you always find sitting together; from jocks, cheerleaders, over achieving nerds, to the basic dorks that found humor in balancing spoons on their noses. Then I spot that there is an empty spot near the back, which I take.

I can't see everyone on the bus; some have their heads down half-asleep, covered by the tall seats that are dull brown and green in color, with the occasional piece of bubble gum stuck to the back. For the most part it is pretty quiet and I don't think that anyone knows that it was me sitting here. I do see some familiar faces, but none to who I find worth talking.

We get to the school about a quarter after seven and everyone races off the bus, pushing and kicking one another, as if someone had set off a bomb somewhere at the back. I wait patiently until it is clear before I make my move down the aisle to the steps and the door. As I walk closer to the exit, I notice a girl sitting in the middle alone, with a colorful wool hat, light blue coat and jeans. She has headphones on, so I don't think she has a clue about any events of the other kids shouting and yelling. I approach her slowly wondering who on earth is this person. I have never seen her before, is it a new student? As I get closer she stands up and I jump back a few inches startled by the sudden motion she has just made. She must have heard my heavy steps because she turns around and looks right at me. She has a face of an angel, dark bangs hanging in her face, the rest of her hair hidden in her hat, plaid shirt and ripped jeans, just enough makeup on highlighting her beautiful brown eyes, with a necklace made of leather with a skull hanging from it. I cannot believe my eyes. It is

Jill! On the same bus as me, sitting alone. I wonder why she is alone.

   She keeps her head slightly down with a small cute grin she waves and says hello to me. Of course I responded, slurring my words slightly as I gazed deeply in her eyes. I mumble, "hello," and ask her what she is listening to, expecting to hear some kind of pop rock band like Nirvana or something , but she responds with Slayer, and in that moment I think we are destined to be together.

   I tell her that Slayer kicks ass and I love them as I follow her off the bus. She doesn't seem at all repulsed by me because she continues the conversation all the way to class. I can't believe my luck that I am walking with her to class. We talk about other bands that we like, such as Anthrax, Metallica, Megadeath, and Suicidal. I cannot believe that we have that much common.

   We have English together first period. I sit a few rows behind her with more than English on my mind. I wonder if that was just a fluke, or is it possible that she likes me. I don't know what to think about all this. I have only had one girlfriend in the past, and that was at summer camp a few years ago.

   I can't resist gazing at the back of her head hoping that she will turn around and give me some kind of sign of her interest. I am day dreaming about what it would be like to hold her hand, touch her skin, wondering what exactly goes through her beautiful mind, what excites her.

   The teacher finally walks in; Mrs. Garland, probably mid-forties, short blond hair, a small woman around the waist, wearing an obvious push-up bra and long flowered dress. She is pretty hot for a teacher.

She starts writing words on the black board about the objectives this year, her name, and what she hopes to accomplish with each student. It is hard to pay attention to what she is saying with my mind racing wild about Jill.

It is nearly noon and time for lunch. Surprisingly, no one has said anything negative about me at all. I wonder if they realize it's me or maybe they are all tired from their exciting summer. I walk outside of the school with my sandwich and sit on the bleachers. Next to the football field where the jocks are playing, tossing a ball around. I am day dreaming as usual, mostly about the strange activities going on in my house. I need to get to the library and see if there is something in there that would help me.

"Hey, what's good?"

I turn around and see Jill sitting behind me. I not sure why she is out here, but she is definitely the best thing I have seen during lunch. I offer to have her sit next me so we can chat a bit more about life. I'm not ready yet to open up to the crazy thought that my house may be haunted.

We discuss more music and how her summer went. I ask her about what sort of other hobbies she likes. We chat about hiking, camping, nature walks and somehow even the subject of cemeteries comes up as we talk. I have a new respect for this person, who I've grown to love from a distance over the last four years. I invite her over to my house this weekend knowing that no one will be home. My parents will go and play their normal poker game with their drunken friends and they will take my little sister with them. My older brother and sisters have their own lives to deal with, so I know they will be out doing whatever suits them.

I spend the last two periods in the library. I am only missing two study halls which isn't anything important. I search the card catalog for any kind of book that would deal with spirits. I want to know if there is a way they could even exist. I can't base my answer on what I read earlier in the bible; that is only one point of view.

I am not having any success, and feel that I should change my research a little and continue on with a more human approach. I think about other phenomena that you hear about such as telekinesis, clairvoyance, déjà vu, and even the ability to read minds and wondered if there could be a connection with ghosts. Is there something within the human mind that could help prove the existence of ghosts? I am able to find several books on those subjects, but very few test cases are reported. I am left with no answers.

I spend the last hour wondering what I can do to figure this out. What kind of devices can I use? These spirits seem to pop up whenever they want. I want to know why, and what they are doing here.

I spend the rest of my week keeping a journal of my thoughts and questions as they arise. I wonder how I will tell Jill about this and what she will think. *Should I tell her?*

It is Saturday night, and as I thought my parents have left to play cards and everyone else went out with their friends. I told my parents that I may have a guest come over for a couple hours, and they didn't seem to mind. At least they didn't give me any negative feedback about it.

It's about 7:00 o'clock when I hear a knock at the door. My mind is racing through thoughts wondering if I should have done more like light candles or start the fire to impress her a bit. We have only chatted at school and joked around a little bit but I want something more. I want to feel her, I want to know that no other soul can ever look at her the way I do.

I open the door exposing her beautiful angelic face glowing from the moon, high and bright. She is wearing a plaid jacket with some regular blue jeans and a t-shirt that pulls tight across her nipples in the chilly air. My heart is racing and I am nervous, hoping that I won't do or say anything that may offend her.

"Hey, how are you? Come in."

She walks through the door and I follow, staring at her remarkably shaped ass from a short distant. I grab her coat from her and hang it up in the game room. My tongue is tied and it is hard getting words out.

I ask her how far away she lives and she says just on the other side of the farm in the small house. She doesn't have any siblings and hanging out is a breath of fresh air.

She notices the pool table and asked if we can play.

"Sure, have you ever played before?"

She says, "A few times."

I have spent many hours playing when I have nothing else to do, and am pretty good at the game. I know that I can't play as well as I am able to after that remark, because I don't want to embarrass her.

I rack the balls up and let her break. She pulls out a pack of cigarettes which shocks me.

"I didn't know you smoked?'

She says, "Yes," in such a soft voice that it makes my heart melt. I reach in my pocket and pull out a cigarette as well, and light one up. I tell her that she can break. She eyes her cue stick and hits the cue ball, releasing the sound of lightning as the other balls bounce off the rails into one another.

I can't keep my eyes off of her, staring at every inch of her body in wonderment and joy. She speaks in a soft, relaxed way and laughs with a small grin as if nothing in the world would matter. I find it hard to concentrate on the game with her in front of me. I move closer to her, hoping for a moment when I can touch her and watch her body move while she lines up each shot.

I can't resist any more, and I just blurt out how beautiful she is. She pauses for a moment with a puzzled look on her face, as if she isn't sure how to respond. *Maybe she doesn't want to hurt my feelings? Maybe she is thinking of a way to let me down easy? What a dickhead I am!* I just know that at any minute she will walk out the door and walk back home, which thankfully isn't too far.

Then she looks up at me, about ready to speak those words that I fear, but know are coming...

"Can we watch a movie?" she says with that same cute grin that I cannot forget.

I gasp as slowly as I can, not letting her know that I've been standing here holding my breath. She follows me to the living room. We put Head Bangers Ball on MTV and watch some kick ass heavy metal videos.

She moves closer to me which is awkward because I don't know how to respond but I think that if blurting out she is beautiful didn't cause her to go home why not try a subtle body touch. I place my hand on her thigh, she placed her hand on top of mine.

"This is a good video" I say as Testament comes on.

"Yea it is"

I lean over closer to her hoping to feel her lips pressed against mine and she does the same. Sparks shoot through me and I think that any minute I am going to wake up in my room with my mom yelling at me.... but that doesn't happen. Her lips are soft and her eyes look more beautiful than ever up close.

I start to rub my hand gently up and down her thigh, feeling the heat generate from between her legs. I place my other hand on her breast massaging it softly, rubbing my thumb over her nipple as I move my tongue down toward her neck. Her hips are quivering and moving with each stroke up her thigh. She wraps her arms around me tightly, breathing hard in my ear while I kiss the back of her neck. *Is this really happening?*

She pushes away from me and I think it is all over, but she takes her shirt off exposing her bra and her beautiful bare skin to me. She pushes me back against the couch and straddles me and starts to kiss me again. I slide both hands down the back of her pants and feel her amazing ass as she thrusts vigorously against my already hard cock. I slide one hand inside her bra and cup her. I ease her perfectly round breast out so I can see all of her milky white skin, then the other. Now I can kiss and lick those nipples that have been teasing me since I first opened the door. I cannot believe that this is happening. I have been fantasizing about this girl for more than a year, and now she is here with me, half naked in my house kissing me.

I can't tell how long we have been here like this but suddenly there is a bang from the game room. *Not now ghost I'm about to get laid!*

She stands up and looks around, "Is anyone else is here?"

"No, we're alone."

"What was that bang?"

"I don't know. Let's check".

I stand up and we walk to the game room. She doesn't bother adjust her bra, or put her shirt back on and she is gorgeous. I turn the light on and that same book has fallen off the shelf onto the pool table again.

I look at her and say it was just a book that fell. I know the mood has left and nothing more is going happen tonight.

We start to hear footsteps upstairs and she is getting scared yelling, "Who is up there! This better not be a prank!"

I say, "No sweetie, no one is here."

She puts her shirt on and follows me up the stairs. I can feel her breath on my back. We get to the top and I turn the light on. We look down the hallway to find no one. I start opening all the doors and turning on all the lights allowing her to check the closets and under the beds. I turn to her and say, "See Hon, there is no-one here."

She asks if she can use the bathroom but doesn't want to do it alone. So I go in with her. I stay by the shower door as if protecting her from anything that may in here. I cannot help but notice how amazingly trimmed and well organized she keeps herself. *Damn ghost!*

After her potty break, she looks at me and says "You wanna walk me home?"

Of course I say yes and we set off by moonlight, walking up the road to her house. We arrive at her doorstep at about 1:30 a.m. I apologize for what happened. She tells me not to worry about it; we will do it again and kisses me softly on the lips as we say good night.

"See you in school." She says.

I spend the fifteen minute walk home floating on air and with a smile from ear to ear. Even though it didn't go the way it could have gone, I will say it was a pretty perfect night. I am pissed at the fucking ghost though and I want nothing more than to see it leave.

Chapter 5:

The Compass

I wake up, eager to go to school on this Monday morning. I want to talk to Jill about what she thinks about what happened Saturday night. I want to know if she believes that there could be the existence of ghosts and if she was really freaked out. The image of her sweet, scared face will forever be embedded in my memory.

I want to hear her opinion on the whole night. I want to know if our moment was a fluke or was it real. I hope it was real. I get my coffee earlier than normal this morning about 4:30 am with my bags ready to go. I start reading more of the Bible and I find several passages that seem to relate to what I am going through.

Deuteronomy: 18,10-12

10. There shall not be found among you any one that maketh his son or his daughter to pass through the fire, or that useth divination, or an observer of times, or an enchanter, or a witch.

11. Or a charmer, or a consulter with familiar spirits, or a wizard, or a necromancer.

12. For all that do these things are an abomination unto the LORD: and because of these abominations the LORD thy God doth drive them out from before thee.

I sit and read that passage over and over, and question what I have become. Am I a witch or wizard that will ultimately be cast aside because of my curiosity? Is what

I'm doing right or wrong? I have no idea. Even though I'm not big on God or the Devil, I've questioned religion more and more these last weeks. I don't know what is going on my house but the research that I can dig up is limited. The selection of books at the school library is minimal, and I will have to go to the library in town to see what they have on the subject.

I set off to the bus stop this morning with only the moonlight to guide me down the road. It is very cold and I can see my breath form clouds from my mouth. I light a cigarette as I wait eagerly for the bus. I am anxious and excited at the same time.

The bus appears in my sight moments later, looking as if it is going in slow motion. Those few minutes it takes to slow down and stop feels like hours and my heart is beating harder than normal, with sweat building in my clammy palms in the cold morning air. The bus stops and opens the door. I flick my cigarette in the field and walk up the steps giving the driver a pleasant smile and nod, as if to say good morning.

I sit right down next to Jill, and glance over to her with a shy smile, I say "Can we talk today?"

"Yea I think we need to, when we can get in a place a bit more quiet"

We spend the rest of the bus ride to school staring at out laps. I want to bend over and give her another kiss but I am not sure if that is what she wants or how she feels. I do gaze in her direction noticing her cute face and angelic eyes. She glances over to me and smiles gracefully as to say we're better than good.

We arrive at the school and wait until everyone else is off the bus before we make our trip down the aisle to the steps of the bus. I let her out as I follow her down. I notice that her ass is shaped beautifully in her tight jeans and her smooth skin show through the rips halfway down her thigh. I fantasize about pulling them off of her and taking her from behind as her ass cheeks sway from side to side as she walks, and her dark hair falls over her back and shoulders.

It's close to lunch and we agree to meet in the library, it will be quiet and secluded. Most people that hang out there during lunch are the hard core dorky readers and they don't like to eaves drop too much.

I get there before she does and start searching the science section for anything that can help.

I find a book about Wolfgang Metzger a German psychologist who lived in the early 1900s. He researched experimental procedures in the world of para-psychology and is well known for The Ganzfeld experiment; which was designed to help prove extrasensory perception which is in short E.S.P., the ability to read minds. I know that psychologists don't know all the capabilities of the human mind, so learning more on topics that most doctors stray away from is, as I've said, fascinating to me.

Jill shows up about fifteen minutes after me. Looking gorgeous as always and finds me in the stack of books. She sneaks up behind me quietly (as if that's possible in a library) and pokes me. I jump, startled and turn around. Before I can say something she wraps her arms around me and kisses me. I know now that I have no need to bring up the topic of us.

She asks what I am doing and I look deep in her eyes and tell her we should sit down and talk. We walk out to the center of library where the tables are and sit down at an empty circular table with etching on it like, the librarian is gay, Mr. Liptz is a fag.

I gaze into her eyes and feel an inner peace about her as if she doesn't care what is going on or what anyone says. I admire this because of my social status within the school. It is at this moment that I know what love is, and how it should be. I think I would do anything she asked for, but I know that she isn't like that at all.

She looks at me and says "What do you wanna talk about?"

"I'm sorry about the odd feelings, and the book that fell, and the noises we heard upstairs."

"Its ok, kind of freaked me out, what the hell happened."

"Brace yourself, Jill."

"I do a lot of different weird research on psychology and have been reading different things in the Bible, I think there is a ghost or ghosts in my house."

"That doesn't freak me out I know you're different and I know that you read books that normally don't get read, I saw them when we looked in your room."

"That's very good to know. I was worried about that. I'm not the most popular kid here, never have been. Actually I think I'm the most rejected kid here."

As she gazes deep in my eyes at that thought and bats her eyelashes, she gives me a cute smile that I have only read about in books and says "I think you're fucking awesome". I am left speechless. I can't get any words out of my mouth. I just mumble and she slides her chair close to mine and kisses me once again.

I look at her and ask what her thoughts on the idea of ghosts. She says she thinks they do exist and that she watches a lot of shows that share different people's ghost stories. I ask if I could hang out and watch one with her. She says sure the next time it's on.

I ask her if she has ever researched things like this.

"No, but could you imagine if we could get one on camera?"

"That would kick major ass!"

One of the jocks comes in and knocks my books off the table, and says "dirt bag" under his breath. I shake my head. *Why me?* I don't do anything to anyone, I keep to myself.

Jill stands up and looks at the guy and says "You're an Ass Hole," then sits back down. She puts her hand over mine and says "Jay, don't worry about that shit. People are just fucking idiots here." I look at her, "Hon, It's all good". *Because right now it is.*

It is the end of the day now, and we we're back on the bus going home. Jill and I sit together, kissing and holding hands all the way home. I know that she doesn't care what people think, and that puts the biggest smile on my face.

My stop is coming too quick and I have to start saying my goodbye to her. I don't want to let her go. I feel as though a small part of me is being torn away, but only temporarily. I know if I really want to see her I can meet her up the road.

I walk up the road to my house, gazing at the sky, as if I finally know what it was like to be in heaven. I don't think I even believe in heaven. Mike Tyson couldn't knock the smile off my face. I have found love and happiness finally, a soul that doesn't judge me for my few extra pounds, my long hair or stoner ways.

My parents come home pissed off at the world as usual, complaining about their dead end jobs that are leading nowhere. I approach my mom to ask if she could pick me up in town tomorrow after school so I can go to the library. Her response? "Get the fuck out of here". My dad sits on the couch watching TV, with the look of pure evil in his eyes, which is normal. I decide not to disturb him. I get a quick ham sandwich and run up to my room.

It is not long before my mom barges in my room and says, "Get up, and get some fucking firewood for the house!"

"Mom, it's eight o'clock at night, the sun is down and I can't see what I'm doing."

Next I know, she sent my dad up, who runs in with his fist clinched and gets me right in my stomach. I keel over in pain with a tear in my eye, and sinister thoughts fill my head. *I want him dead.*

He yells at me and his voice always fills the house with anger. "WHEN YOUR MOM TELLS YOU TO DO SOMETHING....YOU DO IT!" I look up at him and just agree. There is nothing else I can do in this moment.

I spend the next two hours loading the front porch with firewood. I wish they would have had me do this the following weekend. I would have been much more productive. Pissed off and angry, I run up to my room. I grab my compass and my bag of pot. I am going to the cemetery. *Fuck them.*

I storm out the front door without a care for anyone in this house. I sit down in the center of the cemetery which is covered by trees and thick bushes. I know that no one will see me here. I pull out my pot, pack a bowl, and smoke it. Once I'm high, the stress in my life goes away slowly. *Or it won't matter for a while.*

I pull my compass out and hold it in my hand. As always it is pointing north and I am wondering in which direction I should go. I am confused. I know my parents are jerks, but the odd things going on in my house are starting to freak me out and I didn't have a clue what I should do. Jill is not only my best friend, my only friend, but she is also my girlfriend. The night is cold, I have goose bumps and the thick air sends shivers all down my spine. I stare at the compass hoping that it will point toward the path I should take.

I shout out, "Can anyone help me at all? I am lost and I don't know my way?" The needle on the compass bounces and slowly points toward south. My jaw drops. I am shocked, happy and scared all at once. I cannot believe what I just witnessed. Something changed the direction of the compass.

The needle stays pointing toward south until I ask, "Please stop changing the compass direction."

Then it went back to normal. I believe I have stumbled across something that could help me chat with these spirits. I wonder if they can do this, what else can they do. I can't wait to show Jill.

Chapter 6:

OUIJA

According to the Catholic Encyclopedia, Purgatory is "a place or condition of temporal punishment for those who, departing this life in God's grace, are not entirely free from venial faults, or have not fully paid the satisfaction due to their transgressions." To summarize, in Catholic theology, Purgatory is a place that a Christian's soul goes to after death to be cleansed of the sins that had not been fully satisfied during life. Is this doctrine of Purgatory in agreement with the Bible? Absolutely not!

1st Corinthians 12-15

12 Now if anyone builds on the foundation with gold, silver, precious stones, wood, hay, straw— 13 each one's work will become manifest, for the Day will disclose it, because it will be revealed by fire, and the fire will test what sort of work each one has done. 14 If the work that anyone has built on the foundation survives, he will receive a reward. 15 If anyone's work is burned up, he will suffer loss, though he himself will be saved, but only as through fire.

I studied the Bible into the night, trying to find something that could help me more. I found some passages that lead me to believe that there could be a purgatory, but the Bible is pretty vague on that subject, but does suggest one man, not evil or good could still enter paradise through a test of faith after his death, and as I read these scriptures I thought that maybe that's a ghost. Maybe they are just victims of a less harmful fate. I was left with a lot of questions but felt I was on the right track.

I want to indulge my thoughts with some music, so I pick up my guitar and play some chords. The sound I was creating was impressive in my eyes. I put a blank tape in my recorder and was recording the sounds I was creating, while thinking of some lyrics to go with the notes.

My dad busts into my room, and tells me to knock that shit off and go to sleep. I hit stop on my recorder, lie down and close my eyes. It is a cold night and I can see images on my ceiling, projected from my own thoughts. The wonderment of what I now think about life after death is thrilling. I still am not a highly religious person, nor do I want to be, but I know that it did give me insight. People wrote those texts thousands of years ago, and I am positive that they experienced something; what I am not sure, but I am determined to find out. With that thought I drift off to sleep.

I decide to bring my recorder to school o show Jill some of the tunes I was banging out on my guitar, and maybe think of some lyrics. I feel a sense of accomplishment, with visions of standing on stage in front of thousands of screaming fans. Just a childish dream I know, but it is my dream that no one can take away. I don't have any of my homework done because of the hours I spent throwing wood on the porch last night. Before I can explain to the teachers, they are giving me failing grades for the day.

Jill and I made arrangements to meet again at the library during lunch. I spent the hours beforehand getting books pushed out of my hands by some, and others trying to draw on my face with magic marker which was not going to happen. I went out before lunch and smoked a joint in the back of the school. Most teachers can't see back there as the shrubs are tall and cover the windows down stairs, and the windows that are exposed are janitorial windows; and the janitors are more likely to ask you for a hit than to tell on you.

I sit in the library, learning about the idea of E.S.P. and telekinesis when Jill sits down beside me. She tells me that she was looking up some books on early spiritualism, and asked, "Do you know what a séance is?"

I looked at her, "Yea, I've seen them in movies."

"We could do one this weekend at the house. Maybe we can get some answers that way.

I look at her puzzled, "Are you serious with the candles and holding hands," I wink at her and held her hand tight, "and everything?"

"Yes we can make an Ouija board out of index cards, and see what we can conjure up. Maybe it will help you know what is there, and what it wants with you. I don't wanna see you get hurt or anything."

I smile, hug her tight and give her a soft kiss on her forehead.

I ask her if she will listen to the recording from last night. "I haven't even listened yet but want hear what you think."

"What kind of recording?"

"Me playing the guitar. I was messing around came up with some cool melodies I thought you'd like."

Jill places the headphones on her ears and I hit play on the recorder. I can hear the muffled sound coming from the ear pieces but can't hear all that well. *She must be enjoying it because she is bopping her head in time with the sounds I recorded.* I look at her as if I have already become successful in life, as if nothing in the world will matter.

She pauses, and then stops the tape. Her face looks different; extremely puzzled and I can't tell what she is thinking. The only response that comes to me is, "Please. You're not dumping me, are you?"

"Noo. Did you listen to this at all?"

"No. Why? What's up? Does it suck?"

Jill shakes her head, "No, not at all. I like the style."

I am confused. "Why should I listen then?"

"Just do it." She hands the headphones to me.

I put the headphones on, and she hits 'play'. I start bopping my head myself, beating at the strings. There was a slight pause in the music as if somehow the tape was disturbed or crinkled, like someone played a song on a record player backwards. The music got soft, and over the music and noise, was a female voice that said, "Hello, again. How are you?"

I jerk the headphones off of my head. "What the fuck was that? I didn't hear that. My dad came in and told me to stop playing, but that was it."

I now have even more questions. "This thing is moving objects. It's making people feel nervous. Changing the needle on a compass, and now it's being recorded on a tape player. What the hell is going on here?"

Jill immediately looks at me and said, "Let's skip the rest of the day, and to library downtown. We can walk home from there when we're done."

We look at each other, and smile. I don't hesitate to say yes. I only have a math class at the end of the day that I will miss. I can get the work the next morning and finish it before class. I want to learn more about the art of Ouija, and some of the history about it.

We start our walk around at 12:45 p.m. and as long as we were home before 5 p.m., we will be okay. I've made this walk many times before I moved, and the woods were in my backyard now, so I know them like the back of my hand.

The trees are bare and the snow on the path has been well-packed from other people walking on it. I hold Jill's cold hand as we start up the hill through the woods. It is quite a serene sort of peace. I ask her what exactly she thinks could be in my house and whether or not she believes in demons or angels. She pauses for a moment before taking a breath to answer me.

She holds her head down low and says, "I'm not sure. Whether or not we are accompanied by ghost or angels and demons I couldn't say, but that voice on the recorder didn't seem bad. And when I was at your house sure I got freaked out, but I didn't feel like I needed someone to protect me."

"I'm in the same boat. I don't know what it is but whatever it is, I'd like to find out what exactly it is. I've been reading the Bible searching for clues and I'm still clueless. You're right. It doesn't seem bad, just something that's looking for attention. Who knows how long it's been in that house or how it got there. I'd like to know though, Maybe I was supposed to have issues with ghosts to bring us closer together. I have enjoyed every moment we have had together, and every night I go to sleep I pinch myself making sure the day wasn't a dream. To be honest with you, and I don't wanna freak you out at all, so please don't take this the wrong way because I'm not 100% sure yet, but I think I love you. I mean all I see when I close my eyes are visions of your face and the only reason that I keep my head up is you. Even when you smile at me in the hallway as we rush past one another to our next class is forever cherished. But then again it could also be just a stupid high school crush that I know I had last year when I don't think you knew I existed."

She looks and me and gives me a slight hug. I am not sure if I had made a wrong move by expressing myself to her. We become silent for a few minutes, but those few minutes feel like hours before she opens her mouth to say something.

"I do think I love you too. Jay, but much like you I'm not sure what that is. I don't wanna push it but I love hanging out with you. And I do feel comfortable saying you're my boyfriend. I never thought that I would come across someone twisted like me. How many people actually go out and try to find out if ghosts are real?" I hear a chuckle in her voice. I smile back and hold her hand tighter. The mood is definitely picking up.

We get to the library about 1:30 p.m. The main room where they keep the tables is empty. I go to the card catalog and start to search everything on Ouija. I lose sight of where Jill went, but I'm sure that she is looking at books in the ghost section. The library is as eerie as it always is, light dim with just a few on lamps on tables.

Jill's shrill utterance goes up my spine as she races toward me, holding a book on spiritualism. Inside are texts on mediums, empaths, tarot reading, and other forms of psychic abilities as well as witch boards. We sat down side by side and sifted through the book. I want to learn more about their belief in ghosts because I only have a bible to go by so far.

The work of spiritualist Emanuel Swedenborg (1688–1772) and the teachings of Franz Mesmer (1734–1815) provided examples for those seeking direct personal knowledge of the afterlife. Swedenborg, who claimed to communicate with spirits while awake, described the structure of the spirit world. Two features of his view particularly resonated with the early spiritualists. First, there is not a single hell and a single heaven, but rather a series of higher and lower heavens and hells. Second, that spirits are intermediates between God and humans, so that the Divine sometimes uses them as a means of communication. Although Swedenborg warned against seeking out spirit contact, his works seem to have inspired in others the desire to do so.

That little bit of information gives me hope that I am not crazy, and that what is going on in my house may not be evil after all. I look at Jill as she continues to read about different types of entities from the poltergeist (German for 'noisy ghost'), banshee (Irish entity that howls at a moment when someone is about to die, akin to the grim reaper), wraith (the exact likeness of a person also seen before their death), crisis apparition (a figure of a living person normally seen after an accident of some sort, which is a form of astral projection which tells witnesses the person is in trouble).

We finally get to the section on witch boards which have been around for hundreds of years, but were patented in the 1890s by Elijah Bond. It commonly was about a foot or so in length and about a foot and a half wide. The boards were made of wood with engraved letters, a yes and no spot, as well as a spot for a spirit to say good bye. Once Bond commercialized the witch board it was more of a novelty. However, before that point in time they were mostly home made in a similar manner, but were not considered a novelty or toy.

A flat, smaller board just a few inches wide and long, normally in the shape of heart, was called the pancetta, and pointed to a letter or word as you asked questions. All we had to do was put a few fingers on the pancetta and ask questions and the ghost would move it accordingly.

The book also had a warning that inexperienced people should not try and contact the dead with this method, but if you do, to ground yourself with stones, salts, oils, and candles.

I look at Jill, confused and ask, "Are you sure you still wanna do this?"

Without any hesitation she said, "Fuck yes." That's all I need to hear.

We leave the library around 3 p.m. and start our walk home. I know it will take an hour and a half. We take advantage of that time not to discuss ghosts but to joke around and have fun. I kick her in her butt in a comical way and she tugs my hair. Hearing her laugh and seeing her smile is the best thing I have ever seen or heard.

Her house appears in sight, and I assure her that this Saturday will happen, one way or another, and she smiles back. I am excited with hope that we will get some answers, and I am honored, knowing that she will be a part of it. We reach her front door and I kiss her for a long moment and grasp her firm ass in my hands, as we say our goodbyes for the evening.

Chapter 7:

The Opened Door

Saturday was approaching fast I needed to get everything in order with candles, crosses holy water and even started to make my own Ouija board that I was proud of out of some ¾ pine stained cherry and ash letters on it. It was definitely a work of art and I could wait to use it. I met up with Jill Friday after noon just to make sure we are still going to go through with the séance. "Of course." she says.

She asks if she can come over because her parents were going to the city until Sunday. Of course, I didn't have a problem with that at all. We walk up to the house; it is empty as usual and we sit down to watch some afternoon cartoons with bowls of cereal. Woody Wood Pecker cracks me up with the trouble he gets himself into regularly.

She sits on top of me and starts kissing me. I feel the warmth coming through her pants tickling my cock. I grab her ass tight and kiss her neck softly. *I must have of been a real good boy this week.* She leaned back and took her shirt off and I undid her bra and exposed her cute c cup tits and kiss them. She stands up and I follow, taking my pants off and she does too. Her pussy is clean shaved with just a hint of black hair on top of her clit. She kneels down and starts to suck my cock. I grabbed the back of her hair to keep it out of her beautiful eyes.

She stops for a moment and lies down on the couch with her legs open and I have never seen a more beautiful pussy in my life. I kneel down and start to lick her clit, and slid two of my fingers inside of her. She was wet and very warm. I could taste her on my tongue as she moans and squirms in pleasure.

She pushes my head back and I move closer to her face and start to kiss her again, while I slide my cock deep inside of her. I could feel her insides contracting to every push as I thrust deeper and harder inside of her. Her tits are bouncing up and down and I could see her sweat glisten in the sunlight that had pierced through the windows. Her moans sound as though they come from the jungle, like a lion claiming territory. I let out a small moan then pull my cock out of her, and release my nectar all over her chest. She is still squirming and moaning with a slight grin on her face. She looks me in the eyes and says, "Jay, I love you."

I kiss her and hold her naked body close to me. She rests her head on my chest as the credits roll for the cartoon that we started to watch. I kiss her forehead. "I love you, Jill. And I think we should have a shower now."

We walk up the stairs to the bathroom with our clothes in hand. I grab a couple towels out of the closet in the bathroom, and set them on the rack on the outside of the shower door. I turn the water on and we hop in the shower. I allow her to get under the water first. She leans her head back pushing her breasts in my face before she turns and bends over to get the soap.

Her ass pressed up against my cock, I feel myself getting aroused again but we don't have much time before my parents get home. She looked over her should and smiled at me and I can't help but smack her ass. She again grins.

We hop out of the shower and get dressed just in time too, because my mom just pulled up. I put my hair in my hat and we walk downstairs. I look at my mom and say Jill came over to hang out for a bit. She just looks at me funny and says, "I don't care." I know she won't say anything in front of Jill. We tell my mom we are going for a walk.

We go across the street to the cemetery. We walk around a bit and just smile at one another, taking pictures with our camera. She is intrigued by the headstones and we are curious if there is a connection between this place and my house. It is very cold but it is also January. The trees are bare and the road is plainly visible from the cemetery. Jill's hair blows effortlessly in the wind.

We find a fallen tree in the back of the cemetery and sit down. The ground is covered with snow and there is moonlight reflected in it. I want to tell Jill about everything I have been studying, and whether or not it could be useful.

She looked at me and with a soft voice said, "We are in this for the long haul aren't we".

"I think so. There is much out there apparently that I never knew existed."

"Well something odd is going on, we both have witnessed it".

I'm anxious to know, "Please tell me everything that you know, have read or watched".

"Well I'm comfortable saying that you have a ghost. I just don't know what kind of a ghost it is. I hope it's not evil, like biblically evil. But I have heard that most ghosts have some unfinished business, or they're here to watch over someone. Could you picture that, our ancestors watching over us, guiding us through life as if they have the road map to our destiny"?

I laughed, "Well I hope they shut their eyes earlier".

We both laugh. I don't believe in destiny, but somehow I feel as though we were meant to be sitting on that tree, and the moon was supposed to be shining on the snow at that moment. I finally know inner peace.

"Hey, Jill, what do you think about reincarnation?"

"I don't have any thoughts. It is a cool idea I guess, knowing that you die and come back again," chuckling. "That would make us a hell of a lot older than we think we are. I could be like a hundred years old and wouldn't know".

"Maybe that's why we experience déjà vu. Our lives in that past and the present. Basically, we're doing something that we already have done in another life. There is no future just a bunch of past days lined up for us in a row."

I feel more confident as I talk, "I have read that Reincarnation is the religious or philosophical concept that the soul or spirit, after biological death, begins a new life in a new body that may be human, animal or spiritual depending on the soul's previous life's actions. This is a central belief of the Indian religions. It is also a common belief of various ancient and modern religions such as Spiritism, Theosophy, and Eckankar and is found in many tribal societies around the world, in places like Siberia, West Africa, North America, and Australia.

Although Judaism, Christianity, and Islam do not believe that individuals reincarnate, some groups within those religions do talk about reincarnation; such as followers of Kabbalah, the Cathars, the Druze and the Rosicrucians. The historical relations between these sects and the beliefs about reincarnation of movements such as Neoplatonism, Orphism, Hermeticism, Manichaeism and Gnosticism of the Roman era, are connected."

Jill was still looking at me. "You do read a lot."

"Yes, I don't have any friends; you're literally my best friend and only friend. My parents don't even respect me. I feel as though I'm more of a burden than anything to them. Sometimes I sit in my room and tear up thinking about it. All I ever wanted was someone to look me in the face and tell me it's gonna be ok. A hug every once in a while or a good job Jay would be nice. But it's always: do this, do that, get out of my hair, leave me the fuck alone, or someone's pushing my books out of my hand or calling me fat ass, loser or whatever else comes to their mind ".

"Yea, it's ok though they just don't see what I see. You are really an awesome dude and pretty smart. I can't think of any way to make you better, don't worry about that crap Jay. I think you are going to do some great things one day. I admire you, knowing that you push forward everyday going through that".

I want to change the subject, "Do you believe in ancient Indian totem guides".

"I'm not Indian so I have no idea what it is. A spirit that watches you".

"Yea sort of, a totem can be the symbol of a tribe, clan, family or individual. Native American tradition provides that each individual is connected with nine different animals that will accompany each person through life, acting as guides. Different animal guides come in and out of our lives depending on the direction that we are headed and the tasks that need to be completed along our journey. Then there is a totem animal; one that is with you for life, both in the physical and spiritual world. Though people may identify with different animal guides throughout their lifetimes, it is the main guardian spirit and a connection is shared, either through interest in the animal, characteristics, dreams, or other interaction. Gives me hope I guess. Its small little things that make me happy."

"Can I ask you a question Jay?"

"Of course you can, Jill."

"Do you think I have a nice ass?"

I pause in my reaction, I don't know if it took me awhile to process that question or if I was in shock from the question. "I think you have the perfect ass, Jill. I snuggle with that all day long."

It is real late now, probably sometime after midnight, and the night chill has turned to a bone piercing freeze.

We walk back to the house by moonlight. The roads have iced over and become very slippery. Jill holds my arm tight so she won't fall. It is 1:00 a.m. when we finally walked through the door. My parents must have of gone out to a bar or something because the house is empty. My brother and sisters are probably staying at their friends' houses for the weekend as they always do. The house was dark and the energy felt a bit down. I didn't think that anything would happen tonight but if it did I was prepared for it. Jill and I went to my room. I told her as long as we are quit no one would no she's there. We laid in my bed her head on my chest. I just put a nightlight on because it was bright enough to see but dim enough not make anyone want to barge in on us. I could feel her heartbeat against mine and her chest on my abdomen. My arm wrapped around her waist and we fell asleep with a feeling of accomplishment.

We woke up the next day at noon. I asked Jill how she liked her coffee that would go down stairs and make her a cup she said one sugar and milk. When I approached the kitchen my mom was at the table looking a bit annoyed reading the newspaper. She looked at me and said. "How come you didn't send your friend home last night"?

"Her parents went out of town for the weekend and she didn't want to be alone the whole night. So she hung out here we listened to some music and we fell asleep."

"You better not have of done anything!"

"We didn't. As you saw, we were in our regular clothes the whole time."

"When is she going home?"

"Probably tomorrow."

"Ok, you have more wood to stack today and while your dad and I are out playing cards you have to keep the fire going all night it's supposed to get real cold and we may get some snow."

"Ok, Mom. I'll bring wood down. Are the keys in the pick-up truck?"

"Yea but make sure the wheels are locked before you put it in four wheel drive it's been sticking lately."

"Ok, Mom, I'll make sure. It may be freezing up. I'll heat the hubs up a bit."

"Just don't mess the bearings up. They're expensive to replace."

"I won't. What time are you leaving?"

"Around five or so."

"Ok, cool."

I pour Jill and me our cup of coffee and proceed to go back upstairs. I opened the door, and Jill was still lying in bed. I shook her. "Here, hon. Here is your coffee."

She opens her eyes and sits up. I tell her I have to haul firewood and Jill agrees to help.

We are giddy and keep smiling at one another with little words. I can't believe that this is happening to me with Jill. But then again, we are also planning to contact a ghost or whatever it is from another realm later tonight. If everyone at school knew about our plan, they would call us both freaks.

We sit on the couch while we watch the Discovery Channel. There is an interesting show on quantum physics.

Jill looks at me with a friendly stare. Her eyes twinkle in the sun, as it pierces through the window. "Hey, Jay. Do you think we will be together this time next year?"

"I'm not sure, but I hate thinking that we won't. I can only tell you that we will be here tomorrow." Somehow, I think she is content with that idea because she smiles proudly.

"Jay, do you have any plans after high school."

"None at all. Most likely will end up being what is expected of me. I think I'm a failure if you want my honest thought. I have walked this planet doing no harm to anyone. I still get rejected by all. Maybe they see something that I don't. It's a never ending battle that I give up on but it's all good. Want to smoke a joint."

"Please, let's!"

We go outside to the back of the garage. I pull out a joint from my cigarette box and light it up. I take a couple of hits and pass it to Jill. She lets out a cough while she is inhaling. I tell her to take it an easy when she puffs. Her facial expressions say 'don't worry about me, I can handle this shit.'

We get into my dad's truck. My parents are up in their room counting change for the poker game. We drive the truck up in the woods and start piling the wood in the truck bed. We turn the radio and Jill starts dancing in the cold air. She grabbed me by my shirt and pulled me up to her forcefully. We landed on the hood of the truck.

"Jason, get the fucking truck back down here."

"Fuck, Jill! Mom's yelling. We better get going."

We hop back into the truck and drove it back down the hill to the old porch. One by one we throw the logs up onto the porch. We stack the wood neatly at the far back of the porch where it would cover the busted pane of glass. The stack looked unstable, but it kept the wind out.

I start the fire after we had stacked the wood and my parents were walking out of the door. We are finally alone. The worry of someone barging in or yelling my name was gone for another night. I grabbed the blanket that was on the back of the couch and laid it on the floor in front of the fire. I tell Jill it is supposed to be freezing cold tonight, and the fire will take away the chill. She lies down on the blanket comfortably staring in the mirrors and I grab the Ouija board that I had made.

I set the board down next to her, "I made this for tonight."

Her eyes light up as she gazes at the board.

I ask, "Which room do you want to do this?"

"I read that mirrors can help bring in the ghost. I say we do it right here."

"Ok, I'll grab some candles and we can get started."

The environment has changed. It seems dense, but with no fog. The air is thick and unsettling to me physically. I light candles and set them around us.

"Hey I don't know if this would help but when I lived in town I was a boy scout and I keep a compass with me at all times. Last month when I was upstairs something changed the direction of compass. It was thrown off from its magnetic pull. I'm gonna put it down next to the board, as well as the recorder that I got the voice on. It would kick major ass if we got something cool on it.

"That would be cool. I think we should be direct with our questions. I have heard some really bad stories about this board."

I stand up, "Ok let me get a pen and paper and we think about what sort of questions we should ask."

I walk upstairs to my bedroom and grab a pen and note pad. I rush back down the stairs. I can't help but feel as though something was breathing down my neck. The electric charge in the environment feels off the charts. My hair is standing on end. On the right side of the room I see a shooting light, almost as if a star had exploded in the house. A voice whispers in my ear. It was eerie and unnerving. *That has never happened before*. I know that we need to proceed with caution now.

I get back to Jill with the notebook and pen. I tell her about the voice and the light. She looked at me with a look of fear and hysteria. I ask her calmly if she wants to continue and she nods yes. We barely start and weird things start happening. She says she is just as curious as I am and knows that finding out what was going on means the world to me.

We start to write down some basic questions that we plan on asking such as, 'Who are you?'; 'Do you belong here?'; 'Why do you choose to stay in this house?', and so forth.

We place the board in between us and set the pancetta I made in the center of the board. The candles seem to have mystical power because the flames shot up another four inches in perfect harmony. Whatever is there, knows what we are doing, and doesn't appear to have any problem letting us know. I get a bit scared and worried. I don't know what more to expect from this night. I start to wonder what would happen if a demon came through or if this thing was out to hurt us.

My palms are wet from sweat, my vision has gotten a bit hazy, and the room looks as though I am in some other dimension. I feel like I am drugged with some sort of hallucinogenic drug. I feel a bulge in my throat that I would normally feel when I was nervous or edgy. Then I stare into Jill's eyes. She looks as terrified as I do, but doesn't look like she is willing to back out yet. I admire her courage and determination.

****

We asked the first question together:

"Who is here?"

There was no response but Images in the mirror started to form, as though a child started to finger paint, but only in black and white. Some facial features started to appear but were hard to make out in detail. It looked as though something was using the mirrors as a screen for some sort of paranormal projector.

We continued to go through the questions, one at time, allowing minutes to pass in between each inquiry. We received no responses on the board, but our environment kept changing and things were happening around us. Jill looked scared, and her face was pale, and her skin was covered in beads of sweat trickling from her forehead down to her breast.

She shouted at me, "JAY WE NEED TO STOP IMMEDIATELY!"

"Yes, I agree." We took our hands off of the pancetta and said good bye to whatever energy filled the room with us. I turned the lights, on revealing Jill's pale face. Her shirt was covered in sweat sticking to her body. I was eager to hear what the tape recorder may have picked up.

A door upstairs slammed shut as I was making some coffee for us. We looked at each other in wonderment and started walking up the stairs slowly. I didn't know what we would find or what I would do if some weird looking ghost popped out from behind a door. I could feel how edgy Jill was as she walked close behind me holding my arm as if it was a life saving device. Even in this situation, I felt adored thinking that she trusts me enough to do so and I smiled. We reached the top of the stairs and looked down the hallway. Those doors were closed shut and it seemed eerie. The feel of the place was peaceful and happy. I opened each door one at a time to find nothing inside the rooms. We felt relieved and in bad need of another shower.

After our shower we laid in my bed. I was eager to put the tape in and listen. Sure it was only about an hour of recording but knowing what we had just experienced I was excited to see if a voice or noise was recorded.

I asked Jill why she wanted to abandon ship and pack it up so quickly.

"I started hear weird sounds. As if something was trying to whisper in my ear, but too far away at the same time. I felt as though I didn't have control over my thoughts and I couldn't move. I was paralyzed and felt sick."

"Wow, that's weird. I felt a bit sick too, but my vision was impaired as if I was drunk or on shrooms."

I kept the lights on and popped the tape in. I don't know why but all that was on there was white noise. Nothing came out at all. I couldn't hear our voices, noises, creaks, bangs or anything. I was left confused, with even more questions on my mind.

I still had the book from the library, and thought that I would read it tomorrow, maybe there is more insight in there for me. We laid in bed, and fell asleep curled up next to one another.

Chapter 8:

Dude the Clubhouse is On Fire

It's been several weeks since the Ouija board night. The activity in the house has calmed down a bit. It doesn't feel as awkward anymore, and a bit more comfortable in the house. Spring was approaching and the warm weather was creeping up on us. I took advantage of days that reached into the 60s and started to build the clubhouse I wanted to when we first moved in. I gathered every piece of old lumber we had laying around and ripped all the nails out of it. With a rock I started to hammer boards on the tree, building a base for the clubhouse, and then a floor. I took some 8' boards and made walls with some old plywood on the outside. I made it into two levels and on the bottom was a small fire pit with some old duct as a chimney. I took some old mattresses that were made from straw and put them on the second floor.

I spent most of my evenings up there reading books that I checked out from the library. One in particular caught my attention on how magnetic pull works. A magnetic field is a mathematical description of the magnetic influence of electric currents and magnetic materials. The magnetic field at any given point is specified by both a direction and a magnitude (or strength); as such it is a vector field. The term is used for two distinct but closely related fields denoted by the symbols B and H. B refers to magnetic flux density, and H to magnetic field strength. Magnetic flux density is most commonly defined in terms of the Lorentz force it exerts on moving electric charges.

Magnetic fields are produced by moving electric charges and the intrinsic magnetic movements of elementary particles associated with a fundamental quantum property, their spin. In special relativity, electric and magnetic fields are two interrelated aspects of a single object, called the electromagnetic tensor; the split of this tensor into electric and magnetic fields depends on the relative velocity of the observer and charge. In quantum physics, the electromagnetic field is quantized and electromagnetic interactions result from the exchange of photons.

In everyday life, magnetic fields are most often encountered as an invisible force created by permanent magnets which pull on ferromagnetic materials such as iron, cobalt or nickel, and attract or repel other magnets. Magnetic fields are very widely used throughout modern technology, particularly in electrical engineering and electro-mechanics. The Earth produces its own magnetic field, which is important in navigation. Rotating magnetic fields are used in both electric motors and generators. Magnetic forces give information about the charge carriers in a material through the Hall Effect. The interaction of magnetic fields in electric devices such as transformers is studied in the discipline of magnetic circuits.

I also picked up more books on spirituality and other forms of energies. I started to become obsessed with the idea of ghosts and all things that go bump in the night, but I wanted to learn more. I wanted to know why and how. What makes a ghost 'a ghost' and why are they here? I picked up as many books as possible on different religious aspects and started to study the difference between the varieties of beliefs.

In the Muslim world they have the Quran, which Muslims believe was verbally revealed by God to Muhammad through the angel Gabriel (Jibril), gradually over a period of approximately 23 years, beginning on 22 December 609 CE, when Muhammad was 40, and concluding in 632 CE, the year of his death. Shortly after Muhammad's death, the Quran was collected by his companions using written Quranic materials and everything that had been memorized of the Quran.

Muslims regard the Quran as the most important miracle of Muhammad, the proof of his prophet status and the culmination of a series of divine messages that started with the messages revealed to Adam. The Quran assumes familiarity with major narratives recounted in the Jewish and Christian scriptures. It summarizes some, dwells at length on others and, in some cases, presents alternative accounts and interpretations of events. The Quran describes itself as a book of guidance. It sometimes offers detailed accounts of specific historical events, and it often emphasizes the moral significance of an event over its narrative sequence. The Quran is used along with the hadith to interpret sharia law. During prayers, the Quran is recited only in Arabic.

Pagan religions (also Paganism) refers to a group of historical polytheistic religious traditions—primarily those of cultures known to the classical world. In a wider sense, it has also been understood to include any non-Abrahamic, folk, or ethnic religion.

Modern paganism, also known as contemporary paganism, and neopaganism, is a group of contemporary religious movements influenced by or claiming to be derived from the various historical pagan beliefs of pre-modern Europe. Although they do share commonalities, contemporary Pagan religious movements are diverse and no single set of beliefs, practices, or texts are shared by them all. Since the 20th century, "Paganism" (or "Neopaganism") has become the identifier for a collection of new religious movements attempting to continue, revive, or reconstruct historical pre-Abrahamic religion. They are more spiritual and believe the elements of life holds are to be worshipped (Earth, Fire, Water, Air). They believe in respect for all living things and that all have a purpose, such as plants, with healing power physically and psychologically.

I found that it all these traditions are fine to believe but didn't give me answers. My days and evenings were spent obsessing over these questions. I didn't have any answers, even though I had proof. There had to be something, somewhere that could point me in the direction I needed to go.

I went to school studying and researching, and spending as much time with Jill as possible. My one-track mind was definitely starting to take a toll on her. I could tell when the topic came up; she was quick to change the subject and divert it in another direction.

She recommended that I should set up a small party to take my mind off of it. Although the chances of people coming would be slim to none, I still agreed thinking that I just might need to relax a bit. I started to plan on ways to get some beer, weed and other hard drugs.

I spoke with my guy that I bought my weed from asking if there was anything else he had to offer me. He said he could get me some dust that seems to be the new hit amongst teens and assured me I would definitely get laid with it.

The word got out through the halls of our school that I was having a party and had had some good drugs to share. Suddenly I became superman to everyone. They all wanted to attend but I had to keep it down to just a few people. Who would have thought that drugs and beer would make me popular? If it really was that easy I would have of thrown many parties in the past. It didn't matter though as long as Jill was there and I could feel her next to me.

I started hoarding beer that my dad brought home a few bottles at a time. I thought in a few weeks I should have more then 5-6 cases. I planned on having the party up at the clubhouse and felt I needed to find a way to get some electric up there so we can play music. I thought I could put together a couple of 100' extension cords. We that we had some in the garage I could take that night.

The time was getting closer and I was starting to feel a bit more relaxed knowing that I really did need to clear my mind from things. Jill was just as excited as the first the time we hung out. I think she needed a little bit of fun as well.

The day of the party I started to run the chords up to the club house it was a beautiful spring evening, the sun's rays pierced through the trees warming up my back. Jill was there with me, helping out. I told her I hoped it'd be pretty quiet, that I didn't want so many people here. If something went wrong or my parents found out they would whip my ass up and down the road.

My parents took off to go bar hopping I knew they wouldn't be home till around 3:00 a.m. or so. The evening was pleasant there was a breeze in the air blowing Jill's hair away from her face. She never looked so adorable in the whole time I've been hanging out with her. We sat up on the bed of the clubhouse waiting for people to show up.

"Yo, is this the place for the party" we heard outside. We quickly got dressed and yelled down at Brian, a sophomore. He had a crush on Jill but there was no way I was going to let him have a moment alone with her. He was one of the more popular kids in school, always in trouble, spent some time in juvey a year or so ago.

Black hair, leather jacket and he thought he was a bad ass. Personally, I just thought he was an ass.

More people started to show up. People I've never spoken to, much less know their names. Everyone looked like they were having a good time bopping to the music, drinking beer and smoking my weed and dust. Brian kept trying to pull Jill away to have a more personal conversation but I wouldn't allow it. I didn't mind her talking with people but he just rubbed me the wrong way. I already know that the people here never acknowledged me before this party and they only reviewed it as a way to get free beer and weed. Monday morning everything would be back to normal.

Even though it was my party, I was still alienated from everyone else and I didn't want Jill to think it was bothering me. The guests pretty much ignored me and were more worried about doing their own thing.

A fight broke out between two seniors. I have never seen them before. They kept punching one another and kicking, one lost a tooth and the other had a spit on the top of his head which trickled blood every time he turned to swing again. I could tell that they were both inebriated and had no psychological control. We all laughed at the two, wondering what they fighting over.

After the fight I approached the one who got the worst of it to find out what why the hell were they fighting at my house. Apparently, the other guy has been fucking his girlfriend. A big 'no no' in the laws of teenagers. I said, "That's fucked up, man. How do you know? He looked at me and said piss off dip shit." I put my head down and walked away. I started to think that this party was going nowhere in a hurry and began to ask people to leave. I didn't like the idea that I worked hard trying to make people feel welcome, and yet they still call me a dip shit.

Everyone was taking off one by one leaving just myself, Jill and Brian who was searching for a Walkman. I said, "How the fuck can you lose something like that. Didn't you keep it in your coat?"

"I was on the bed when it went missing. Do you have a flashlight?" Before I could respond, he grabbed a candle I had on a shelf and crawled under the bed with it.

The mattress caught fire and the three of us trapped ten feet in the air. I turned my back to see where Jill was, and she looked terrified. I looked back at Brian and the whole wall was already up in flames. I knew the ladder was on the other side of the wall and I needed to get everyone out safely. I charged the wall and broke it down. I told them to get out of the way. I threw the mattress out the window, scorching my hands on the springs and jumped out of the club house.

I looked at Brian and said, "You better grab an end to this mattress and help me drag it down the road to the brook." He took off in the woods and ran home. I drug the mattress to the brook. By the time I got back to see if Jill was okay, the flames were out from the fort and fire trucks were starting to drive up the road.

Jill was sitting with her head in her lap. I asked if she was ok.

"Yea I'm fine. I'm sorry about all this. I didn't think that this would happen."

"It's ok, babe, not your fault at all. We just got to get this cleaned up the best that we can before my parents show up."

I wasn't worried about the club house just the trail I left to the brook. That was pretty noticeable. I could clean the club house tomorrow and no one would no. We went inside the house, cleaned ourselves up and sat on my bed. I looked at her and gave her a hug.

"I understand why you wanted to have a party, and your right I do need to think about more things than what is going on this house. We need to get out more and do other things."

"I was hoping that people would see you for the cool person you are. I wanted to do something and have fun. I hate knowing that we are just subjected to ghosts and hanging out in your house. There is a whole world out there and different adventures at every turn."

"It will be ok. I promise."

"I hope so. I love you Jay, and I want to have a fun future ahead of us." I held her tight not wanting to let go. I started to notice a change in us that I didn't like.

I hated feeling that distance between us and knowing that deep inside the fate of our relationship was doomed. I didn't want that to happen. My emotions ran wild, more concerned about my path and direction in life more than anything. I wasn't sure where I was headed. I had no friends; my girlfriend I feared was starting to resent us as a couple. My grades in school weren't the best but that was my own fault. My parents treated me as a burden more than a blessing.

I planned on making some major changes within my life and needed to seriously start to think about where to start. I felt as though I had lost sight of who I am and my ambitions. What really did drive me to keep going? I didn't want to become a victim to everyday society and try to fit in a social class that clearly doesn't want me. Most of all, I didn't want anyone to be drug down with me. I seemed to have forgotten all that was paranormal for that moment, while Jill lay in my arms. Emotions ran wild, cutting every inch of my nerves, and I didn't want to accept any of it. One day, I would have to be something big. I will look down at the past with pride and forgiveness for those who have mistreated and belittled me life. For now I will press forward and change what I can.

"Sometimes people let the same problem make them miserable for years when they could just say, "So what."

"My mother didn't love me." So what.

"My husband won't ball me. So what.

"I'm a success but I'm still alone." So what.

I don't know how I made it through all the years before I learned how to do that trick. It took a long time for me to learn it, but once you do, you never forget." Andy Warhol

Chapter 9:

The Empty House

Making plans for the following weekend was tough. Knowing what to do was the problem. All I could think of was to walk to the next town, which was only a few miles away. There was a path that I could take. I had never been on it yet but exploring new territory would be pretty cool. Obsessing over ghosts has eased a bit, and I've started to get in my daily routine. I became a servant to the yard work brought on from Spring. The weather was fairly warm and was it comfortable wearing only a t-shirt and some jeans. I still saved my notes on the phenomena that have been happening and from time to time I would open them, but really haven't pursued further research, though it has been on my mind.

I felt confused and extremely disoriented, wondering what I would become and how my relationship with Jill would turn out. She had been my best friend this whole school year and I admired everything that she has done for me. This was the first time I felt loved and the first I seemed to have walked with a purpose.

I spent a lot of time in the library during lunch with Jill reading typical books on human development and behavior patterns. One of the biggest things I learned was how your social class affects your behavior. If you were to hang out with criminals, chances are you will become one and so forth. That knowledge had me wondering if that was my problem. My obsession with paranormal phenomena. People don't think that ghosts exist, just as most people didn't care if I existed. It seemed to make sense to me. There hasn't been extensive research in this genre of science that I have seen, only books based on faith and belief, as well as some movies.

I looked over at Jill, who was sitting across from me, and I asked her if she wanted to walk into the next town over this weekend and see what's happening there.

"Sure I bet we could have some fun out there."

"Not sure if there is a party or not, but it will be something new."

The silence was deafening and that about killed me. I didn't like the short conversations. I felt as though the knife was already in my gut, just waiting for someone to grab it and turn. I felt alone again and knew I needed to fix it.

I wanted to make an impression this weekend, and somehow I knew I could. I spent the rest of the school day in an emotional state of solitude. The week passed without incident. My work around the house was fairly caught up and didn't have much to do Saturday or Sunday. My parents decided to stay in that weekend (I suspect they were broke). The only concern I had at that moment was making an impression that would secure Jill's love. It was a quiet evening until the phone rang. I was expecting my weed guy to be calling, letting me know that he received a stash. It was him, and not only did he get a stash in, but he had some tickets to a concert that I wanted to go and he was willing to give me the tickets, because the band wasn't his brand of music and he couldn't sell them. The concert wasn't for a couple more weeks, which would give me plenty of time to find a ride. I'm sure I could convince my mom to drop me off in Middletown. Worst case I would walk. Two tickets were perfect; Jill and I could both go.

There was a knock at the door. I knew it was Jill as she had phoned me earlier. I had thirty bucks in my pocket, and knew it would come in handy during our journey to Florida, New York.

"Mom, Jill and I are walking to town."

"When will you be back?"

"A few hours, probably around 8:30."

My parents for some reason had grown fond of Jill and she had no problem with us walking to town. We headed up the road, past the cemetery that even in the spring was hard to see due to the over brush. Still, all in all, it looked just as peaceful as the day I discovered it. I thought for that moment that I should dedicate some of my time to cleaning it up.

"Hey Jill I got tickets to the concert in a couple weeks. I would really like it if you could go. We just have to find a way there."

"Really? That is awesome. Of course, I wanna go. I heard that shit is gonna kick some ass."

"Sweet this is gonna be awesome."

There was a change in the way she spoke after that. That look and sound of excitement ran back through her and I was pleased to see it. She smiled again, like the angel I remembered, and I gazed into her eyes feeling as though I had accomplished something big. All I ever wanted out of life was to feel like I was approved of, and it never took much, just a simple gesture was more than satisfying.

There was an old age home about a half mile up the road. It looked as though it had been run down but was still in use. Multiple massive buildings stood on the grounds that filled the space on the black dirt region of the county.

I felt the urge to find out what was on Jill's mind and I needed a way to bring up that particular discussion. We walked along the back half of the old people's home, down a narrow path that I'm sure would lead to town. "Hey Jill I wanted to apologize to you."

"For what?"

"I know I've been obsessed with this whole ghost thing, and I know that there is a life outside of that which you want. Not sure exactly how to put it in words, but I have noticed that for some reason it seems different for us. Almost like we are growing apart." A tear ran down my face, but I still kept my composure. "I really hate thinking about that and if there is something that can be done please let me know."

"It's not you, Jay. It's more me. I know what you're talking about and I am sorry you feel that way. I've been in the dumps lately. My parents are getting a divorce and I know my world is going to change. I'm not sure where I'll be in a few months or even who I will be with."

"I'm sorry to hear that. Wish my parents would get a divorce and send me to some boarding school or orphanage. You mean everything to me Jill and I want you know that you have done more for me than any other person has ever. When I say I love you, I really mean it. I'll remember our time always."

The trail started to narrow just barely giving us room to walk side by side. The trees were overlapping above our heads, letting in just a few sporadic beams of light from the sun's rays. It was a soothing feeling, and couldn't be more perfect. The scent of lilacs and wild rose filled the air along that narrow path, bringing a new pleasant feeling and mood between Jill and me.

Along the path we noticed many buildings. One however, seemed a bit isolated. Why would a building be by itself in the middle of the woods? The roof had cedar shingles, broken and sunken in, probably from the elements. The siding was intact, covered in chipped white paint exposing some minor holes that animals had burrowed through. The windows were broken, exposing wall studs and broken sheetrock. There was a porch on the side which looked as though it was used as the main entrance. The lawn didn't look like it had been mowed for years. I was intrigued by this house, and something drew me too it. I needed to get inside and look around. I was curious if anything was left inside. I was pretty sure that a farmer had lived there being that we were smack dead in the middle of farm country New York. Everyone here pretty much is farmers whether it be corn, onions, pumpkins, celery, potatoes, or live stock.

I looked at Jill and asked if she wanted to go in for a bit and look around. She seemed just as interested as I. We walked closer to the front door, taking in the view from the outside. I wasn't sure if it was something paranormal or just the condition of the house that sent shivers up my spine, but it felt a little unnerving.

"Jill, we better be careful going in here. I don't want us getting bit by any animal that might be in there."

"Yea, I know. It's just a creepy building."

We approached the front door slowly, only to find that it was barely attached. The door leaned inwards. The single pane of glass set in the door was cracked. The floors looked unstable, dusty, and sunken in some spots. The hardwood boards was starting to separate from each other. Even though the tension of fear ran up our spines, I still felt at home for some reason.

Step by step we slowly walked the halls, watching out for any signs of animals that may have made this building their home. Dung from smaller animals like raccoons, mice and bobcats covered the floors. It wasn't a good sign but those animals are typically harmless, more likely to run from you than attack.

We heard a loud thump upstairs and immediately went to investigate. We crept up the stairs slowly, trying to avoid putting too much pressure on each step. My main concern was falling through the floorboards, and getting seriously hurt. There were separate landings in-between each floor, changing the direction of the steps. It smelled very musty and as if this was a public urinal. Some kind of framed art hung on the wall of the first landing, although I couldn't make out what it was through the layers of dust. We reached the top, which exposed and elbow-shaped hallway. I looked at Jill and she seemed content and giddy. Her eyes glowed with excitement in a peaceful way.

"Damn, Jill this building is a wreck."

"Yes, I can't see why anyone would wanna be in here now."

"Maybe a homeless person getting out of the cold during winter. I'm sure no one is in here now."

We didn't hear anything else from inside the building. We ran through the hallways, flinging open each door, checking out what was behind it. The toilet had a turd left in it and jokingly I look at Jill and said "you hungry babe". She ran down the hallway, shouting at me, "Come find me, babe". I laughed and set off to look for her, peeking in each room saying, "Are you in here?" in a devilish, playful way. She made the mistake of shifting her weight in a closet she was hiding in and knocked over a board. I quickly ran to that room and grabbed her, threw her over my shoulders and laughed, "I got you! Ha, ha, ha!" while I spanked her ass.

I carried her back down the stairs and put her down in the kitchen, where an old table was sitting. She grabbed me and started kissing me. Her shirt came off before I had time to think about it. She cleaned a spot on the floor afterwards, and just wanted lay down next to me. She had silent tears in her eyes.

"You ok hon." I said pulling her close.

"Yea, just thinking about my parents."

"I'm sure it will be ok. You will still get to see them both. Just not every day. Besides you now get two Christmases, birthdays, etc."

She smiled, as if to say, 'You're right, but that isn't what I want.'

"I know it's just tough."

She squeezed me tight.

"GET OUT!"

"What the hell was that?" Jill gasped.

"I don't know, but wait here."

I reached in my back pocket and pulled out my compass. I walked the building with caution. That voice sounded like it came from inside.

"Who is here?" I demanded.

"Why are you here?" Again demanding.

I wasn't getting a response. I kept asking for whatever was there to come out and talk. I said I wasn't afraid of it, that this wasn't the first time I've been in this situation.

My compass started spinning, then slowing, pointed to a corner of the living room. I looked up and said, "I may not be able to see you but I know you're there. Please tell me why you don't want us here, and why your still here."

Jill let out a slight scream. I ran to her side and grabbed her.

"What happened?"

"There was some fog that swirled. A hand reached out." You could hear fear in her voice as she trembled.

"Let's just leave."

We walked out of the building slowly, Jill was holding me tight and I could feel her trembling. We walked away from the building a few hundred feet before calmness came over us and she stopped trembling. I didn't know what was in that building but I truly believed that I handled the situation the right way.

She didn't want to continue the journey. Instead she just wanted to go back to my house and relax. I had never seen her that scared before and wasn't sure how to handle the situation. We walked back down the path, headed home with the sun starting to set; orange, yellow, and red rays of light piercing through the trees with a majestic view.

Chapter 10:

The Break In

The school year had gone by quickly and there were only a couple months left until summer. I started to appreciate my present life a little more, knowing that what's coming after seems to be a permanent prison filled with jealousy and regret. Jill and I have been spending our weekends together whether at my house or hers, despite her parent's personal issues. They seemed to have accepted me a little and I appreciated that reprieve.

I have grown emotionally and learned to not let anyone beat me down. I thought of the Jill's words, "You're going to do some great things Jay." I repeated those words over and over in my head. Alone or not, I know I will be happy and successful. What direction I was headed was still unclear but I did have a knack for science.

I spent much of my time learning that consciousness is the quality or state of being aware of an external object or something within oneself. It has been defined as: sentience, awareness, subjectivity, the ability to experience or to feel, wakefulness, having a sense of selfhood, and the executive control system of the mind. Despite the difficulty in definition, many philosophers believe that there is a broadly shared underlying intuition that is consciousness.

Philosophers since the time of Descartes and Locke have struggled to comprehend the nature of consciousness and pin down its essential properties. Issues of concern in the philosophy of consciousness include whether the concept is fundamentally valid; whether consciousness can ever be explained mechanistically; whether non-human consciousness exists, and if so how it can be recognized; how consciousness relates to language; whether consciousness can be understood in a way that does not require a dualistic distinction between mental and physical states or properties; and whether it may ever be possible for computing machines like computers or robots to be conscious.

At one time consciousness was viewed with skepticism by many scientists, but in recent years it has become a significant topic of research in psychology and neuroscience. The primary focus is on understanding what it means biologically and psychologically for information to be present in consciousness—that is, in determining how the neural system and psychological system correlates of consciousness. The majority of experimental studies assess consciousness by asking human subjects for a verbal report of their experiences, i.e., 'Tell me if you notice anything when I do this." Issues of interest include phenomena such as subliminal perception, blind sight, denial of impairment, and altered states of consciousness produced by psychoactive drugs or spiritual or meditative techniques.

The end of another weekend was quickly approaching, at the end of a hot month of May. I was eager to just relax and watch TV. I didn't have anything on my list of chores. Winter was over, so no more fire wood was necessary. The yard was mowed and cleaned up for the week.

I rented a couple of movies that I thought Jill and I would enjoy, like Indiana Jones, and another action comedy. My parents were planning on going out for the evening to some bar to listen to some country band play. All I knew is that they wouldn't be home until about 3:00 a.m.

I prepared some snacks like sausages, cheese, crackers, soda, and popcorn to enjoy while we watched the movies. We haven't really spent much time inside lately, mostly walking the streets and hanging out at the mall in Middletown.

My parents left sometime before dark and Jill arrived shortly afterward. My parents knew she was coming over and I was happy that they didn't mind. We shot a game of pool and listened to music to start the night. We blared some Iron Maiden and drank a case of beer, joking around and having some fun.

I loved seeing her smile as I made sexual innuendos with the cue stick. She would stand behind me, which I have to admit was kind of a turn on. I started to feel a bit light headed probably from the beer and sat down in the chair that we had by the pool table. She came over and straddled and started to ride me as if we were in a strip club. She whispered in my ear. "Do you like that"?

"Fuck, yes!"

I grabbed her hips and helped her thrust alongside of my cock that was throbbing by now. She got off and took my pants off and started to suck me off. I gazed at her while her head moved up and down while I had her by the hair.

"Take that whole dick."

"Let me know when you're going to cum, hon."

"You know I will."

She moved faster and faster. I couldn't contain myself any more I felt the urge, that tickling sensation at the head of my dick that all men love to feel. "I'm getting ready to cum, babe."

"Just for you Jay, I love you"

"Love you, Jill. That was so amazing. Thank you."

"You're welcome," she winked at me and walked upstairs.

I yelled up at her while she was in the bathroom. "Hey, hon, I've got some movies for us to watch."

"Ok, I'll be down in a few minutes."

I went into the living room and lit the candles. I pulled out my bong and started to pack it. She came down and sat next to me, and said, "I hope you have enough for me."

"You know, I do babe. I've selling this pretty fast so I......have been getting a lot of the good shit."

She smiled at the notion and took the first hit. The water gurgled and she pulled the smoke through the pipe into her lungs. She started to cough as the smell of roses left her mouth.

"Told you I got the good shit. I may hit up some shrooms this week. That should get me some extra cash."

"That you did. It is some good shit. When do you plan on getting the shrooms?"

"Probably the middle of the week. Let me make some coffee so were not too Chinese-eyed when my parents get home."

I perked a pot and handed her a cup. I packed the bong one more time just to ensure that we were just as relaxed as ever."

"Thank you, Jay."

I popped in the first movie. I don't think it would have mattered considering that we were dangerously stoned by now. The theme music played in the beginning and Jill said I love this fucking movie. I just smiled at her with a look of hope on my face. She curled up next to me and snacked on the snacks that I had gotten for us.

We didn't finish watching it before our eyes had closed. Thankfully there was a blanket that my mom loved to have on the back of the couch. There was a slight chill in the air so a light blanket was somewhat needed.

BOOM!!!!!!!!

We woke up startled, wondering what the hell was that noise. I got up and told Jill to stay on the couch. I walked in the garage and grabbed a tire iron from my dad's tool box and started to make my way through the house. I looked at Jill and she had a frightened look on her face. I just said, "Stay put. The phone is on that stand." I didn't see nothing out of order on the main the floor. So I carefully walked up to the second floor. I flung every door in the hallway open not seeing anyone in the rooms. The only room I couldn't get into was my parents which they always padlocked whenever they left. They never trusted any of their kids as if they had something special in there, worth a million bucks or something. I ran down to the basement but didn't see anything unusual. I was left wondering, what the hell was that noise. *Where did it come from?* It sounded as though someone knocked over a dresser or something really heavy. I was puzzled and confused.

I called the bar where my parents were and explained to them what happened. That we fell asleep watching "Indiana Jones" when we heard the bang. I told them I searched the house and didn't find anything at all. They said they were on their way home.

I was left puzzled. Jill looked scared and I wasn't sure how the night was going to end. I had no idea where that sound came from or how it happened. We sat on the couch with the lights on trying to keep our nerves from exploding. I could tell she was afraid. I asked if she was okay. She kept saying, "Yes." I held her close to me.

My parents arrived about 45 minutes later. They glared at us as if death was in their mind. The tire iron was still beside me. The coffee was still hot, so I poured Jill and I each a cup. My dad started to search the house for anything out of the ordinary much like I did earlier. I don't know what that bang was but I was eager to find out.

"JASON GET YOU ASS UP HERE!!!!"

I walked upstairs knowing that didn't sound good. I didn't know what to expect when I got up there but apparently I was in trouble. I reached my parents room and walked inside to find both my parents staring at me with a look of hate. My dad grabbed me by the shirt and drug me over to the closet. The shelf had broken in half. Everything that on the shelf was now on the floor, and a small dresser that they had in there was knocked over. They asked me if I did this.

"No dad, how the hell am I going to get in your room? You lock the door."

"Well, somebody did this. "

"Dad, I don't know who did it. Maybe the shelf gave out and knocked the dresser over."

He looked at me puzzled, knowing that I was right. They did lock the door and I had no way into their room. I knew that there was no way that the shelf could have knocked the dresser over, and I believed that my dad knew it as well. Maybe the ghost struck again, but I wasn't sure. He let go of shirt and said, "Jill can't come over next weekend." That *hurt worse than a beating*.

I walked back down stairs and sat beside Jill. I had some more research to do at school on Monday. Jill looked at me worried and confused. She whispered softly in my ear, "You want to go somewhere to talk?"

"Yea, let's go outside."

I grabbed another cup of coffee for myself and asked Jill if she wanted another cup. She nodded and I poured her one too. We walked across the street to the cemetery. I asked out loud without expecting an answer. "Why does my life suck?"

"Your life doesn't suck. What did your parents say?"

"The shelf in their closet busted in half and the dresser in there was knocked over. Somehow they think it was our fault. They said you can't come over next weekend."

"That's bullshit. You can come over my house and hang out there for the weekend."

"That's not the point Jill. We didn't do anything. They don't have to take it out on us. Their room was locked, and there was no way that we could have of gone in there."

"I know. But your parents are douche bags."

I chuckled at that notion and agreed.

"I'm now left with more questions that I don't have answers for. I don't know if the ghost decided to come back or not, but it seems that he did."

"You may be right. Not sure. I understand you do have to get some of this crazy shit figured out. Jay, just promise me you'll be careful. Ever since that Ouija board I have had nothing but bad feelings about you contacting this things."

"I promise. I won't do anything stupid. I'll proceed with caution."

I went to the library looking for any book that could help me figure out how a ghost could do this. It would have taken a lot of energy to break a shelf in half. I ran through the aisles, throwing book after book in my arms; anything that could help me. I started to read one on poltergeist ghosts.

In folklore and parapsychology, a poltergeist is a type of ghost or other supernatural being supposedly responsible for physical disturbances, such as loud noises and objects being moved around or destroyed. Most accounts of poltergeists describe movement or levitation of objects, such as furniture and cutlery, or noises such as knocking on doors. Poltergeists have also been alleged to be capable of pinching, biting, hitting and tripping people.

Poltergeists occupy numerous niches in cultural folklore, and have traditionally been described as troublesome spirits who haunt a particular person instead of a specific location. Such alleged poltergeist manifestations have been reported in many cultures and countries including the United States, Japan, Brazil, Australia, and most European nations, with early accounts dating back to the 1st century A.D.

Chapter 11:

Strange Shadow

The physician John Ferriar wrote an essay on a theory of apparitions in 1813 in which he argued that sightings of ghosts were the result of optical illusions. Later, the French physician, Alexandre Jacques François Brière de Boismont published "On Hallucinations: Or, the Rational History of Apparitions, Dreams, Ecstasy, Magnetism, and Somnambulism," in 1845, in which he claimed sightings of ghosts were the result of hallucinations.

Joe Nickell, of the Committee for Skeptical Inquiry, wrote that there was no credible scientific evidence that any location was inhabited by spirits of the dead. Limitations of human perception and ordinary physical explanations can account for ghost sightings in his opinion; for example, air pressure changes in a home causing doors to slam, or lights from a passing car reflected through a window at night. Pareidolia, an innate tendency to recognize patterns in random perceptions, is what some skeptics believe causes people to believe that they have 'seen ghosts'. Reports of ghosts "seen out of the corner of the eye" may be accounted for by the sensitivity of human peripheral vision. According to Nickell, peripheral vision can easily mislead, especially late at night when the brain is tired and more likely to misinterpret sights and sounds

I spent a lot more time reading and researching different types of activity from reports across the globe. I found that I was not alone. Other people have seen and heard similar phenomena. The term 'possession' was thrown around a lot, and that definitely raised my awareness, and encouraged me to proceed with as much caution as possible.

Possession doesn't just happen. There are stages that are involved, according to researches and priests of the Catholic Church. Typically, demons choose their victims wisely and single out the weakest of a group. Apparently, the weak are easy to manipulate and it doesn't take much to turn that good soul to a sinful one. Lucifer doesn't want to kill the soul; he wants to recruit members for his army is the belief. This leads me to believe that a demon's sole purpose is getting their subject to turn against the light or god. But I don't think that a demon, or Lucifer, really cares whether or not I believe in him.

Regression is the first stage. In order to understand regression, one should think about its opposite, which is progression. If you're not progressing you're regressing, meaning moving forward and backwards. Demons pick out people who are not progressing in their religious beliefs, so they were considered an easy target.

The second stage is repression, which according to demonologists is the outward sign that regression is happening. Victims tend to be joyless, miserable, and unhappy. I thought my parents were repressed when I was reading this.

The third stage is suppression. The subject strays from his or her true emotions, bottling them up. Normally, a demon tends to start to take control of the person in this stage. This is not possession yet as it's still not within the victim. The person could still get help if they choose to do so, and could ignore the discreet voice of the demon which whispers in their ear.

If the victim doesn't get the help they need, the person sinks into an all-time low of depression, and believes that they are worthless. The victim feels they have been kicked to the ground and will do anything to get back up again. Feelings of being unloved and unwanted flood their heart, making them easier to take over and more desirable to the demon. They start to do as the demon pleases, looking for some sort of acceptance which brings us to obsession; which is exactly what it says. The person becomes obsessed with breaking God's commandants, inflicting self-harm, etc., out of hate for the holy one above; blaming God for their circumstances.

Finally there is possession. The soul is no longer pure, and thus perfect to recruit for the Devil's army. The victim is now ready to meet the evil one and be brought into the fiery blaze of hell.

Exorcism, from the Late Latin: exorcismus—to adjure, is the practice of evicting demons or other evil spiritual entities from a person or place, which they are believed to have possessed. The practice is quite ancient and is still a part of the belief system of many religions.

The person performing the exorcism, known as an Exorcist, is often a priest, shaman, or an individual thought to be graced with special powers or skills. In general, possessed persons are not regarded as evil in themselves, nor wholly responsible for their actions.

The concept of possession by evil spirits, and the practice of exorcism, originated in prehistoric shamanistic beliefs. In Hinduism, the Vedas, which are the holy books of the Hindu religion, include sacred spells needed to cast out demons and evil spirits. Several examples are found in the Hebrew Bible, and the New Testament includes numerous exorcisms among the miracles performed by Jesus. Today, Catholicism, Eastern Orthodoxy, and some Protestant sects recognize the practice.

In recent times, the practice of exorcism has diminished in its importance to most religious groups, and its use has decreased. This is due mainly to the study of psychology and the functioning and structure of the human mind. Many of the cases that in the past were candidates for exorcism, are often now thought to be the product of mental illness, and are handled as a medical condition.

I found myself becoming more and more of a detective as the weeks went by, searching for facts and not relying on belief any more. I did have an obsession with the subject but it never took over my life. I thought about all the knowledge I gained from the books and the discoveries I made with my compass and recorder.

There were groups out there that look into these ghost stories and use more specific equipment such as dowsing rods, Geiger counters, and radiant air meters. I thought for a moment that I could do that. Either way, I had started on the journey and that thought put a smile on my face.

I called Jill up conveying the information that I had been reading. Telling her about possessions, spiritual beliefs, and different sort of gear people were using to document paranormal activity. I wasn't sure exactly how the equipment worked, but I was excited knowing that I wasn't alone. Jill had become not only a major inspiration but a major part in everything I was learning. She was seemed a bit happy to know that I was starting to understand the strange happenings that were going on in my house, and was supportive of all that I was doing.

For some reason I laid in bed that Thursday in late May, feeling a sense of insecurity. I missed Jill even though we would see each other the following day. I couldn't help but envision how she was lying in bed, probably with one of my shirts on, which she would always steal from me. I didn't mind it, but was a bit frustrating when I went to look for a specific one and it was gone. I thought about how limp her body was while she slept. How her smile shined with a light so bright it could only be compared to that of a morning sunrise in the summer. Her body was perfectly shaped and her heart was as big as a zephyr.

I couldn't help but get aroused thinking about her. I knew we would have sex tomorrow during study hall. Which was turning out to be an everyday thing. I wondered why she loved a person like me. I know that I'm no one special, and I have strange and weird hobbies which she now was a part. In my eyes she could have of had anyone in school but she chose me? I don't know why but she did, and I adored her for that decision.

I went downstairs to smoke a joint and get a nice huge bowl of Cheerios. I walked outside. It was quiet with everyone asleep. I heard the usual footsteps pacing down the hallway on the second floor, which confused me because no one else heard them. They must be heavy sleepers I think. The door going to the basement would close from time to time, sometimes fiercely, as though someone slammed it during an argument. I chuckled. *It must be a woman.*

The night was warm and the stars shined brightly. I pulled the joint out of my cigarette pack and lit it. I sucked in the smoke, filling my lungs as I watched the head burn, glowing brighter the harder I hit it. I could feel my head start to spin and any stressful thought that was in me was gradually sifting away.

I felt a poke from behind me and I jumped, startled not knowing who it was. I thought maybe the ghost was starting to become physical and I was worried. I turned around slowly to find Jill there, in tears.

"What's wrong, why are you here this late?"

"My parents are arguing. My dad is moving out this week. Can I stay here tonight?"

"Yes, of course you can stay. Where is he moving to?"

"Middletown. with my uncle."

'What started the fight?"

"Money. Money fucking sucks Jay. That's the cause of most fights."

"I know what you mean. Want some of this joint."

"Yea, I'll have a few hits."

"You can get on the school bus with me. I think you should call your mom up though and let her know you're here. I'm sure both your parents are worried about you right now."

"I will in a bit."

She took the joint from me and took the biggest hit that I had ever seen her take. She was hearing the footsteps that I had been telling her about happening almost every night. She looked at me surprised she was hearing them and said, "Is it safe to be here with that going on?"

"Yea, I'm used to it. Hear it every night. Can't figure out what the hell they are pacing for, but they don't bother anyone."

She smiled and hugged me. I could feel her worry, her anger, and depression. I gave her a kiss, softly on her lips, as she stared at my face.

"Everything will be okay."

"I know, one day at a time."

I grabbed her hand and escorted her up to my room. She put on one of my shirts to sleep in. I stared at her and said, "Jill, don't ever walk here by yourself again. Please call me up, I'll be more than happy to go to your house and walk with you."

She apologized and said, "Yes I know. I'm sorry." I smiled at her and kissed her forehead. I had no urge to have sex. I held her close as we fell asleep.

We woke up a bit late that morning, giving us about a half hour to get our clothes on and to head out to the bus. My parents were already gone and must have noticed Jill in my room because they left me half a pot of coffee. We just made it down the hill when the bus was stopping. The door opened and we jumped on. The bus driver smiled and said, "Long night?" I said, "Sort of."

We got to our normal seat and sat down. I told Jill she had to go home tonight at least for a bit to talk with her parents. I didn't think that it would be fair to have them worry about her. Even though they didn't like me I still showed them the respect that they deserved. She said that she would and then come over afterward.

I could tell through that day that she was scared and nervous. I did everything that I could to keep her smiling, but that was harder than I thought. I would hand her some sweet notes and even some sexual cartoons. Each time she responded by giving me a small grin as if to say thank you but that isn't helping. I felt helpless, not knowing how to cheer her up. I threw her a note explaining that I could see she wasn't okay and maybe we should just go and hang out up in the woods until school was over. She was happy at that thought and agreed.

We left school at lunch. It was easier then because most kids were allowed to leave the school property and all we had to do was blend in until we reached the opposite side of the parking lot, then walk right into the woods up the hill. We reached a clearing which had several oversized rocks big enough to fit a few people on each laying down. I pulled the soda out of my back pack and drank it. Jill got undressed down to her bra and panties. I looked at her and smiled.

"What the hell are you doing?"

"I'm going to work on my tan."

She laid out on the rock with her back exposed to the heat of the sun's rays. I finished the soda and started to poke some small holes in the top of the can with a little knife that I always carried around. Why I carried that one I have no idea; the blade was barely 2 inches long and couldn't protect me from a water pistol.

I laid some pot over the top of the holes. I sucked in through the mouth part. I looked at Jill and asked if she wanted a hit.

"Yea, I do."

She grabbed the can from me and took a nice long hit. I finished the rest and laid beside her, rubbing her back. I could tell that she was starting to feel a little better, as she moaned slightly at every pressure point. I didn't want to have sex. I just wanted her to relax.

I glanced down at my watch and saw that we only had about 45 minutes left to get to the school to catch the bus. We ran down to the school just as the other kids were walking out of the building. Our bus was parked right next to the woods. I said she needed to go home and come back to my house around five or so. She agreed, and said, "Don't worry, babe. I'll be there. Be sure you're ready for me though." and she grinned.

I walked through the front door of my house and threw my bag on the couch. I made half a pot of coffee for myself. The TV had been left on for whatever reason. White noise filled my ears from the empty channel. The cable box must have been turned off. I went to shut off the TV when I heard a female voice speaking with emotional intensity.

"HELP ME, PLEASE."

"What kind of help do you need?"

"Please, help."

I was confused. I didn't know who was speaking or how. *How was I going to help something that won't give me an answer on what they wanted?*

"WHERE ARE YOU?" I didn't know where to turn or what direction to go. I really did want to help but felt useless.

"What do you want? Please talk to me some more. I'm not afraid, please don't be afraid of me either."

Still getting no more responses, I was worried, scared and concerned at the same time. I didn't hear this female voice when I heard it on the recorder. This was a new one.

I heard some shuffling in the game room and I quickly ran to go see. There was nothing out of place and I was starting to panic a bit. I could feel my heart beat in my chest as if it was going to explode. My mind was racing, not knowing what was going to happen or how to predict what she was going to do.

"Hurry! I'm trapped."

"Where the hell are you, ma'am. Please help me. I can't see you, and I can barely hear you."

I wasn't getting any responses to my questions, and fury, and impatience were starting to take over my emotions. This wasn't good, I thought that this could be a bad thing.

I turned and look at the stairs. Something told me I needed to go up there. I didn't know why or how I felt the urge to, but I know I needed to go up there. I could barely breathe in the thick air that surrounded the game room. My nerves were on end and my hair was standing up.

I walked cautiously toward the stairs. I stopped in front of them. My chest was hurting. It was hard to breath. I gazed up wondering if I could make it to the top.

One step at a time I went up the stairs. I was worried, concerned for my welfare and scared. My skin was pale, and I felt nausea. I was determined to find out what help was needed and who was in trouble. The temperature dropped, my breath was almost visible on this hot day. A rush of air ran past me, as though I was standing still alongside of the highway. The window halfway up the stairs was blacked out for a moment and the second of darkness made me wonder if I was a subject of possession. I felt as though the grim reaper was breathing down my back and there was nothing I could to protect myself.

I looked at the top of the stairs, to see a black human-shaped mass glaring at me. He didn't have to say anything or make any gesture for me to know what he wanted. I knew he didn't want me or my family there. I knew his intention was to ensure that we were out of that house one way or another. I knew he would subject all of us to force if necessary. I was frozen in place. My stiff limbs couldn't move no matter how hard I tried. I thought for a moment that this was not the way I was going to go out. I shouted at the man.

"We are not leaving! This is our house. You're no longer welcome here. You have done your time. You must find peace within you and learn to forgive yourself."

He lowered his head slightly as if he was mocking me, and turned down the hallway and walked away. I felt my body starting to become mobile and stumbled up the rest of the stairs. There was no sign of where he went. Not a trace of what I had just seen. I felt more worried and confused. Somehow, this ghost must be stopped, but I didn't know how. I finally saw the spirit that had been pacing the hallways, and knocking books over. The more I thought about it, the more I believed that he was just mocking me. But this wasn't his house anymore and it was time for him to move on.

"Honey?"

Jill was here. I didn't think that it was five yet. My parents would be home in about an hour.

"I'm upstairs. Can you bring me up a cup of coffee?"

She walked through the door holding her clothes and jumped on top of me. I watched her tits bounce up and down as I sucked on them. She seemed better and I was happy knowing.

We lay in bed naked. After a while, I told her about what had happened before she got there. She looked scared a bit and just as confused as I felt. I sipped my coffee and told her that everything was going to be okay. *I'll figure it out.*

It did freak me out, but I refused to let it get the best of me. Somehow, I thought the ghost knew that as well. I truly believed that whatever, or whomever, wanted to just scare me. I was determined to find out why.

Chapter 12:

The Eviction

Jill had come to grasps with what I have been going through and seemed a bit more determined to find out what was going on. We compiled more data that we gathered from books. The term energy has been widely used by writers and practitioners of various esoteric forms of spirituality and alternative medicine to refer to a variety of phenomena.

Such "energy" is often seen as a continuum that unites body and mind. It is sometimes conceived of as a universal life force running within and between all things, as in some forms of vitalism, as a subtle body. In Chinese medicine as qi, and in Indian yoga as prana or kundalini. Sometimes, it is equated with the movement of breath in the body, sometimes described as visible "auras", "rays", or "fields" or as audible or tactile "vibrations". These are often thought to be perceptible to anyone, although this may require training or sensitization through various practices. The term "energy" also has a scientific context, and the scientific foundations of physical energy are often confused or misused to suggest a scientific basis for physical manifestations, properties, detectability, or sensing of psychic energy and other physical phenomena, where no presently known scientific basis exists.

Still a bit confused on what exactly could fuel this phenomena, I wanted to learn more about natural conductors. Whatever this was had been here for a while and there had to be something on which it used to survive. We started to look at our surroundings and what we knew was here. We had the cemetery, which included dead bodies as well as headstones. The caskets under the ground were probably tin, or wood.

There was also the rock quarry that was just through the woods. What kind of materials would they have there? I know they used explosives, heavy machinery, and large motors. Or could it be something else? I needed more research. I needed to look at it from a more spiritual side again, and the power of stones kept getting thrown around in my head.

The electrical conductivity of cylindrical cores of Westerly granite, Indiana limestone and Nugget, St Peter and Kayenta sandstones was measured at about 25°C in vacuo, in air, and after saturation in distilled water, tap water, and 0.1 MNaCl solution. The three-electrode technique with a guard ring and the two electrode technique without a guard ring were used. Core aspect ratio over the range of 2.00 to 0.25, as well as frequency over the range of 50 Hz to 10 kHz, influences the conductivity of all rocks, especially those measured in vacuum. Measurements from water-saturated samples using a guard ring are not appreciably different from those obtained without a guard ring. The conductivity of rocks saturated in 0.1 MNaCl solution changes least with a change in aspect ratio; for these rocks a linear relationship, known as Archie's Law, exists between log porosity and log conductivity. No simple correlation was found between those factors in rocks saturated with tap or distilled water. Thus, it appears Archie's Law is of questionable value for correlating laboratory data from rocks saturated with low-conductivity fluids.

The quarry had a lot of limestone and quartz, which has similar properties. Could this be part of the fuel as well? I wasn't sure but I truly did believe that we were on the right track.

We started compiling all the experiences we had in the house from when I first moved there. I kept mental notes of each encounter including the one that my sister told me. I wanted to figure out the best way to capture this ghost. I didn't want a belief such as Catholicism or Spirituality to cloud my mind in any way. I wasn't sure who had the right answer, but I was determined to find the answer. Everyone seemed to have their own thoughts and ideas. But no one had any proof, so in my eyes they were ideas, not fact.

Jill and I decided that we alone were going to camp out one night taking pictures, using the tape recorder, and checking to see if something could also manipulate my compass again. We wanted to plan everything out with as much detail as possible. We knew there was going to be risk involved and that something bad could happen at any time. Jill recommended that we study on certain ways of protecting ourselves from harm.

We learned that for Protection from negative energies, stones to use are black kyanite, black obsidian, black onyx, bornite, celestite, citrine, elestial crystals, jet, katanganite, kunzite, peacock ore, plancheite, quartz, schorl or black tourmaline, smoky quartz (especially in healing). That was what we needed.

Black onyx wouldn't be a problem. I was sure we could get that from the school. We felt fully prepared for this and that we knew enough to do what was needed. I became more and more excited over the idea of finally seeking the truth.

That Saturday came and Jill had the look of pure excitement in her eyes. I haven't seen her like that since the first time we had sex. I loved that girl more than anything.

The phone rang for my parents. I didn't hear what was being said but they didn't seem happy at all. I prayed that whatever was going to happen tonight, that it wasn't going to break or destroy anything. The punishment for that was something that I don't think I could bear. My parents left, spinning tires out of the driveway shortly after that conversation. I wasn't sure what was going on, but knew finding out was just a matter of time.

Jill and I started to go over our plan. We agreed that we would spend a sufficient amount of time in each area of the house, including the basement. We thought that it would be best if we stayed together and remain as calm as possible.

My expectations for the night weren't too high. In all honesty, I really didn't expect anything to happen but I was hoping. I made some fresh coffee and got a blank notebook. I wanted to have notes of everything that happened. We sipped our coffee and kissed. Something about danger was a massive turn on. I didn't want to smoke any pot that night either. I thought being under the influence would affect the results.

The sun was going down pretty quickly. One by one we shut each light off in the house, hoping that the dark would bring the ghost out to meet us. The night was quiet, but we felt as though we weren't alone and that whatever was here was watching us closely.

We stepped outside to have a cigarette. Jill's face glowed like an angel in the moonlight, and I couldn't imagine feeling more at peace. I grabbed her hand and asked if she was ready to start. I could tell that she was nervous, and a bit worried about what would happen throughout the night. I smiled at her gracefully, with confidence that we were safe.

Our first stop was upstairs. We thought that we could spend a half hour up there then move downstairs. She sat at one end of the hallway and I at the other. The recorder was placed in the center of the hallway and I held the compass. We were only about twenty feet from one another and I could see her silhouette from the moon shining through the window just above her. Even though I had another purpose tonight, I couldn't help but to be aroused at her perfect shape.

I started off by being polite, assuring that we had no violent or harsh feelings for the entity. We didn't want to upset him or make him feel as though we were trying to dominate him in anyway. *When I saw him a week ago he didn't seem too friendly. I wasn't sure why, maybe he thought that we are a threat to him. That wouldn't explain the female crying for help though.*

"Can you please tell me who you are?" The silence was deafening. We could have heard a pin fall in the living room at that point.

"Do you want to be left alone?"

"Who is the female that needed help?"

"What kind of help does she need?"

"Do you feel trapped here?"

There was a bang downstairs. I didn't know what it was, but it was pretty loud. Jill was startled by the sound. Some kind of ball of light shot down the stairs toward the game room. I looked at Jill and said, "We've got to go check that out."

I got up and walked toward Jill grabbing her hand to help her to her feet. We walked downstairs, slowly listening to each stair creak from the weight of our bodies. The light orb was gone. It had disappeared without a trace. I grabbed my camera and started to take pictures, one after another, of the game room.

Jill noticed while my camera was flashing that the book fell off the shelf again. Same book every time, the holy bible. I wondered what its problem was with this book I thought. The night was still young and we had made some serious progress so far and were I eager to try the questions down stairs. Static charges filled the air. I knew we weren't alone, but I was confused, wondering why this entity wasn't revealing itself.

One at a time, I repeated the questions. Listening intently to any possible noises. There was no sound at all. I hoped that a voice came over the recorder. Jill started to calm down a bit and no longer looked scared. That worried me a bit, not knowing if she would scream, run or just freak out. I didn't want to show fear tonight, and her reaction in the abandoned building when we took that walk wasn't exactly comforting.

We took our first break of the night. I turned the lights on in the kitchen expecting to see some kind of ghost glaring over my shoulder. But there wasn't one, just Jill standing behind me with her arms wrapped around my waist. I filled the coffee pot with more water and fresh grounds, and stepped outside to discuss with Jill about that first half of seeking answers from the unknown, while the coffee brewed.

"How did you feel that first half?"

"I felt good. Excited about the second. I thought that something was whispering in my ear the whole time we were upstairs."

"Really? That's awesome. Nothing really happened that I can recall. Just the book that fell and the ball of light that went downstairs. I thought that was strange and odd. I hope we got a voice on the recorder."

"That would kick fucking ass."

"I wanted to say thank you, Jill, for being here with me."

"Anytime. That's what I'm here for, right?"

I smiled at that and nodded in agreement. I pulled her closer to me with my arms wrapped around her waist and embraced her energy with mine. She looked up and kissed me ever so gently on my lips. I wanted to take her in every way possible. I felt so aroused by her looks and touch, it's hard to control my emotions for her.

We went inside and sat on the couch with some coffee, as headlights pulled in the driveway.

"Shit, my parents must be home. Its only midnight why the fuck are they home so early?"

"I don't know."

"They left the house earlier pretty quick. I wonder what's up, either way the rest of our night is shot."

They walked through the door and just looked at us. They didn't say anything but I could see disgust and anger in their eyes. I wasn't sure if it was directed toward me or not, but they ran upstairs and just went to sleep. I popped in a movie and cuddled with Jill the rest of the night. She passed out pretty quickly and I soon after.

I woke up early the next morning feeling as though every ounce of energy was taken from me, as if I hadn't slept in weeks. No one was up yet nor was there any sign of life within the house. I didn't know why I was up so early. On the weekends my eyes usually wouldn't pop open until at least noon and here it was 6:00 a.m.

The coffee never smelled better. I don't know why this morning was any different nor did I care. I needed that boost. My mom walked in the kitchen shortly after it was done.

"Jay, we need to talk."

"Ok, about what?"

"Yesterday, the landlord called. He says that he owed back taxes and was forced to give up the house. We have a short time before we have to move. So I am telling you that you have to start getting ready for that."

"We just got here under a year ago. I hate moving. I just got fond of this place. Why the hell does this always happen. What the fuck am I going to tell Jill?"

"I don't know son, but it's got to happen."

"Where are we going?"

"We will not leave the school district. We don't want to change that. That wouldn't be good."

"Thank god."

I turned my back and stared at Jill. Depression sank over me. She was all that I lived for and I didn't want her to feel disappointed in me. I knew that I would have to tell her, and soon. I was felt scared, worried and nervous all at the same time. I looked at my mom and told her when Jill wakes up tell her I will be right back. I need to go for a walk.

I left the house in a hurry. I didn't expect her to wake up anytime soon. I walked through the woods and up to the top of the cliff at the quarry. The sun was coming up and reds, oranges and yellows filled the horizon. I needed help and guidance. I needed serenity.

I was angry at the world; hatred ran through my blood, filling the arteries that just hours ago were tranquil. I sat down and cried with my head in my hands. I didn't want to leave. In the beginning I hated this house, wanted really nothing to do with it. But I thought back over everything that happened, all of the knowledge that I had gained, the fun that I had, and for the first time I felt respect from someone.

I moved into the house feeling rejected, not caring about what happened to me and alienating myself from the world. I had no self-respect or esteem for that matter. I walked aimlessly without direction or hope of a brighter future for myself.

I don't have the popularity, but I do have a sense of direction. I know that the sky is the limit with my future. I don't care what people think about me now, and walk with a purpose. Jill was right, one day I will do some amazing things and my life will forever be changed because of her.

I hope that we can still be a couple and if not, I hope that she finds happiness with whomever she chooses. Some people say that things happen for a reason, or that people are placed in your life for a reason. I know why she was sent to me and will always love her for that despite any outcome.

The spirits in the house also had an impact in my life, despite their creepiness, and some morbid ways. They taught me to understand and know that not everything is as it seems. Even though letting go of the past may be hard and challenging at times, it's not worth being stuck in the past. All it will do is eat at your soul every day and fill your life with hate and anger. That was a sentence that I wasn't willing to serve.

A warm breeze went up my spine at that moment and I knew what I had to do. I knew it was time to tell Jill, and hope that she would feel the same way. This won't be the end of us just another obstacle to hurdle, and new adventures to pursue.

About the Author:

Jason Stanton is a radio show host, paranormal investigator and paranormal researcher from Wurtsboro Hills, New York. Jason's background in the paranormal began in 1992 with an accidental EVP (electronic voice phenomena) he recorded while playing music at a cemetery near his home. He also noticed that a compass he placed on a headstone was pointing to the wrong direction. This occurrence led to an ongoing and ever expanding study of magnetic fields as pertaining to the paranormal. Jason lectures on his findings which have grown to include radiation, parapsychology, geomagnetic field and electromagnetic radiation. Ghost Chat Radio started in January 2012. This fresh and edgy 2 hour weekly show has been a huge success with as many as 70,000 listeners per show. Jason set a record with that number for internet paranormal radio and has also been nominated for 2 awards by the New England Paranormal Awards hosted by C.C. Huntress. Jason continues to work to raise the bar. Jason Stanton has been interviewed on Fox Radio Network, London Knights, Family Spirit, and more. Jason was a speaker recently at Dixie Ghostland Paracon in Aiken, South Carolina. Jason Stanton Co- Founder of Eternal Dead Paranormal and lead investigator.

Made in United States
North Haven, CT
31 May 2022